A W̶ ̶ ̶ IN THE RAIN

by John Davis

in accordance with the Dream

First paperback edition April 2022

Book design by Publishing Push

ISBNs
978-1-80227-464-6 (paperback)
978-1-80227-465-3 (ebook)

Published by PublishingPush.com

A WALK IN THE RAIN

Foreword

This book is an imaginary walk with people and characters from the past, starting from the 1950s. I hope you will find it amusing. The names of the villages have been changed. In those days, most people were known by their nicknames. During this walk, I will discuss the secrets of life which I have been shown in dreams and spiritual teachings. This may help you understand the true meaning of life and why it appears to be unfair, with some people having good lives and others having horrible lives. It is all in accordance with the Dream.

A WALK IN THE RAIN

Contents

Foreword... *iii*

The Dreamer .... *vi*

Chapter 1: Is There a Creator?.. 8

Chapter 2: The Dreamer.. 15

Chapter 3: The Creation of Opposites.. 20

Chapter 4: Consciousness 24

Chapter 5: The Divine Gem... 28

Chapter 6: The Percentage of the Opposites 32

Chapter 7: The Master of the Dream and its Opposite 36

Chapter 8: Where we come from and where we go.................................. 40

Chapter 9: Level of Consciousness.. 44

Chapter 10: The Workings of the Maze 47

Chapter 11: Free Will... 51

Chapter 12: Speed of Light.. 55

Chapter 13: The Purpose of it All.. 59

Chapter 14: Water Skiing 62

Chapter 15: Looking down through the worlds.. 65

Chapter 16: The Second World.. 68

Chapter 17: Looking at the Traps.. 71

Chapter 18: More of the Traps..74

Chapter 19: The Turning Point 77

Chapter 20: Some Spiritual Interests..80

Chapter 21: The Secret..83

Chapter 22: Explaining the Master of the Dream 86

Chapter 23: Trust It..89

Chapter 24: Dreams..92

Chapter 25: End of the Walk, Beginning of Freedom 95

A WALK IN THE RAIN

The Dreamer

by John Davis

In the silent darkness there lies a thought

and into life you were brought.

All that was meant to be

was created by the power of three.

Sound and Light are Its tools

for those who know these are the jewels.

Things are not what they seem;

we are ALL in the Dreamer's dream.

Why are we here? many ask.

To find the answer is your task.

It's not so hard if you are keen;

call the Master of the Dream.

He'll meet you in that silent dark;

from then on, you will never part.

If its truth you have sought,

give this a careful thought.

The sustaining power from above

is the power known as love.

If It didn't love its dream so dear,

all creation would disappear.

Come with me on this walk;

we can laugh and have a talk.

Never mind the wind and rain;

you may never think the same again.

Now there's a thought!

A WALK IN THE RAIN

Chapter 1

Is there a Creator?

As I look out of the window, the dark, dismal rain clouds hurry past, driven by a gusty south west wind, and disappear behind the trees on Abbot Hill. I remember, as a child of 10, squeezing myself inside an old car tyre and rolling down the hill, then getting out at the bottom staggering like a drunk until the giddiness wore off. The rain taps on the window, then slowly slides down the glass onto the stone windowsill before dripping onto the ground, the end of its journey. A bit like us, really, at the end of our journey; we end up in the ground one way or another. Or do we?

My thoughts drift off to some warm and sunny beach and clear blue skies. Who needs the rain? My eye falls on the flowers in my small but well-stocked garden. They look a picture when the sun shines on them. What did I just say? Who needs the rain? Of course – life does, for without it, what would there be? Just a bare desert. Life – now there's the mystery, with all its many forms and complexities ever struggling to survive.

Come on, let's put our macs and wellies on and have a walk in the rain. I can tell you as we go what has been revealed to me about life and some of its hidden mysteries by the Master of the Dream – because things are not what they seem. I must close the gate or nextdoor's dog comes in and buries his bones. Look out! That was Rusty, Albert's Alsatian that's just rushed past chasing Blacky, the Post Office cat. Look at them both sliding on the wet pavement as they round the corner, oblivious to us or the rain. See the village ducks waddling across the road and plopping like floating corks into the pond at the edge of the green. Their ducklings almost run to keep up and then throw themselves off the bank into the water, huddling round their parents.

Now here's a point worth thinking about. All life reproduces itself – animal, vegetable and mineral. Let's sit in the bus shelter for a moment and have a ponder on sex and reproduction – I see your eyes lighting up – for if ever there was a miracle, this is certainly one. Life is sacred, but alas, most people pass through it without a thought, just to live and die. Let's take the time to look at life, and please keep an open mind.

All life on this Earth has the ability to reproduce, and in some species, there appears to be some form of love, whilst in others, it is just an act of sex. But this reproduction must have been there at the very beginning of life when primitive life forms were first created. Now this is the question for you to think about: was life created or was it by accident? Maybe there's another slant to this question you may not have looked at. It could be that life needs a form to live in and it was the form that was created. If this is the case, life is one all-embracing thing, whether it be in a fish, tree, man or worm, and it is the form that has been created by life for life. One thing we must agree on, that there must be some form of intelligence connected to these phenomena of form and sex. Now scientists are beginning to unravel and understand the formation of DNA, the building blocks of the form, so even the scientists must agree that intelligence must have been involved. This takes us back to the question "accident or design?". There can be no doubt it was not by accident as this would be impossible; therefore, there must be a creator in one form or another.

This leads us to another question: "Why a continuation of the form and life?" This must have been planned because of the unique and complex way the form is recreated for life to control it. This brings us to the most important point to consider: "Are life and form two separate phenomena or are they one?" If they are one, where has the life force gone while the form is decaying after death? The energy needed to control the form cannot be destroyed, so it must be a separate phenomenon to the form. At this point, it would be logical to consider yourself as not the form but the energy that controls the form. In simple terms, you are life.

The rain has eased off, so let's walk up to Ted's farm as there's a lovely view over the valley. Mind the car! Oh look, here comes Charlie on his bike. He weighs 22 stone, so you can imagine the spokes in the wheels straining with every slow push on the pedals, which give a worn squeak as they cry out for oil. Notice how he slides from side to side because his saddle is too high; he almost falls off before heaving himself upright, only to topple over the other way. His cheeks are puffing out as if he is blowing a trombone, and every time he pushes the pedal down, he lets out a strange sound as though it is his last breath. It is dangerous to walk out in front of Charlie because you never know which way he's going to go! Because of his slow pace he can hardly balance, so he wanders all over the place; you would think he is following an imaginary zigzag path.

"Morning, Charlie! How's the wife?"

"Huh, fine, sent me to get some, huh, vinegar."

Even his voice is slow and melodious. With Charlie safely out of the way, we cross the road, go over the old wooden sty and walk along the path to Ted's farm. Some lovely wild flowers in the hedgerow are bobbing their colourful heads in the breeze; there is something wonderful about spring. It is very strange, you know: Ted is a very large man with big chubby cheeks and his wife is also quite large, yet their two sons are tall and thin!

The amazing thing is that we are all different, not only in looks and build, which are connected to the form, but our character and personality are also unique and are connected to life, which is the self. All the millions and millions of people in the world are all different. This also applies to the animals and trees. I wonder if it applies to cows? Ted reckons he knows every cow by name, although they all look the same to me, but it is this unique difference which is part of the mystery of life.

How are you finding the climb? Fortunately, Ted keeps this footpath in good repair, filling the holes with shingle. Notice there are quite a few mounds of dirt made by the moles. They are funny little creatures, spending life digging underground and annoying gardeners and farmers alike. There's a reservoir over there behind us, but those trees hide it from view. We may go that way later.

Well, here we are at the top. I need to get my breath back! It's quite a climb. I used to run up here when I was a lad and fly my kite with the other boys from the village. We had those stunt kites with two strings so you could make them go left or right, up or down. We used to try and dive-bomb the cows until MacNally dive-bombed a bit too close and his kite got stuck on a cow's horn! Mick Cason plucked up enough courage to tell Ted. Luckily the string broke as the cow danced around the field, shaking her head trying to get the kite off her horn.

We are all different, and the form or body is designed especially for each person or creature, so life can experience a variety of things. You must realise that life existed before the form was created, so if you were wondering where we have come from and where we go after we die, I will explain that later, but there is much to understand first.

Ah, the sun's just popped its head out of the clouds for a moment. Over there, by that clump of trees, you can see a ray of sun shining like a giant torch-beam. We'll take a walk through the woods in a minute when I've got my breath back.

Talking about the sun, it's a strange thing that although the sun is hot, the higher you go in a plane, the colder it gets. If this was not so, the Earth would be much hotter and wouldn't support life; therefore, this was by design. Look at the universe: all the planets are in their own organized orbits, each held in place by magnetism. This would certainly suggest that there is some intelligence with the ability to organise.

Are we ready? Mind you don't slip. Would you like a peppermint? They warm the insides!

You may be thinking, "Why create a planet that can support life in its various forms in the first place? Is there a motive?" Trouble is, our lives are so short that it's hard for us to comprehend time on a large scale. But over a vast period of time, life within its form has evolved into some amazing life forms, indicating that life has the ability to adapt and to diversify. This can only be done with intelligence.

It's started to rain again. We'll turn right by the oak tree, where the squirrels have a great time collecting the acorns in the autumn to store for the winter. We'll go down Pinks Hill through the Lower Woods. We used to play Cowboys and Indians after school in the summer. Kids don't play like they used to, stuck indoors with their phones and computers. We tried to see who could climb the highest in that old silver birch. Bryan Clark tore his school trousers one day and his father gave him a good walloping! These woods haven't changed much over the years. The path may be wider, but that's all, really. Those bluebells look like a moving carpet as the wind ruffles them in sea-like waves. What's that? Over to the left, there's a squirrel darting across the path and climbing up the horse chestnut tree with the grace of a ballet dancer. It flies through the air and lands with the precision of a fighter pilot on the overhanging branch of the next tree, its bushy tail swinging from side to side like a feather duster flicking the dust off the branches.

The Creator most certainly has intelligence, and life has intelligence. This would suggest that the Creator and life are closely linked or are even one consciousness?

12

The biggest fear man has is death. How do you feel about it? Don't like to think about it? I know how you feel. This may be because you view yourself as the body and not as life. Trouble is, everything that has life must leave that form sometime. Those with strong religious beliefs are not so scared of death, but modern people are becoming more skeptical of religion. Slowly man is turning away from spiritual thoughts and concentrating on material wealth.

Here we are at the stream. Mind how you cross as this old plank can be rather slippery. There used to be stepping stones, but too many people fell in so they put a plank across. Listen! A woodpecker! How on earth do they hit the tree so hard and fast? They sound like a pneumatic drill! You would think they would bend their beaks, but apparently they have a shock-absorbing joint in their head. I wonder how long it took for that to evolve and what happened to the first one? I bet it had a headache!

You will find that the more man turns away from his spiritual self and the Dreamer, the more society will slowly deteriorate. Law and order will become harder to achieve.

Hey, there's the Mudhole! Well, the real name of the pub is the Red Lion, but the locals call it the Mudhole because before they put the drain in the road, every time it rained hard the water would run down the hill and into the pub. They would open the back door to let the water run out, but when the water had gone, the floor was always covered in mud! Come on, we'll cut across the field! They do some nice toasted sandwiches in there. It's amusing what names people call things; even some people's names are funny. I met a young man on holiday once whose name was Dwaine Pipe! His parents certainly had a good sense of humour, and that's a good thing sometimes. We had a boy called Hugh Shore in school, but they moved some years ago.

Here, we'll climb over this gate. Don't worry, the cows won't hurt you. They may follow us, but that's all. We'll have a drink and something to eat while we discuss some spiritual viewpoints which you may find somewhat contrary to mainstream understandings. Sometimes it is good to break old moulds because it can disrupt complacency, and if you have not been interested, a new point of view may make you sit up and look. It's all down to the Dreamer.

A WALK IN THE RAIN

Chapter 2

The Dreamer

*Y*ou can get a better look at the Mudhole if you come here. Mind your head on the low-hanging bough with the water dripping off its leaves in a rhythmic pattern. Notice the building is leaning as though it is tired of standing there for all these years and slowly falling asleep. From here, it looks as though that big oak tree, with its large, strong branches, is holding the building up, but in actual fact, it is about 20 feet away. It was a doodle bug in the war that made it lean like that when it landed in Watson's field opposite. Let's get over the style and cross the road here. Look how much water is coming down the road; although it's not raining that hard, there is a small stream already!

I'll wipe my boot on this mud-scraper outside the door. Notice how even the doorway is lopsided. They had to get Two-planks to make a door to fit. He's the local carpenter. They called him Two-planks at school because he wasn't very good academically, and the name has stuck! Mind you, he's a good carpenter and has done well for himself. It's quite a cosy old place, with the ancient oak beams and horse brasses hanging from them. Each design has its meaning. People took a lot of pride in their work in those days. Those strap things hanging down from the beams are for the drunks to hold onto, to stop them falling over!

See all those mud stains on the flagstones! They won't have carpet laid in case the drain blocks and the pub floor gets flooded again. I'll have a shandy and a toasted cheese and tomato sandwich, and you have what you fancy. Let's sit over by the window; there's a nice view down the lane.

You may be wondering why I mentioned the Master of the Dream, and this should become clear later. Before we start discussing creation, it is important that you try to accept that all creation is only a dream and the Creator is the Dreamer. Everything is created out of Light and Sound; to us, it appears as solid, but in reality, it is not. It is only energy which is agitated by magnetism. The more it is agitated, the more solid it appears. As we progress, you should understand how the Dream is created and why it is described as a dream. I hope we both agree that there is a creator and, therefore, Its sole function is to create. There is a more important reason, which we will come to.

The first thing the Dreamer needed to create was a substance to construct and bring Its dream into being. The Bible gives some clue to this where it states, "In the beginning was the Word," but mathematically and geometrically, it would appear that Light could have been the first creation and geometrically influenced the creation of the Word. There are indications that this Word was HU, but I will call it Sound to avoid any misunderstanding. Light and Sound are, therefore, the key to all creation. Light and Sound, although separate, are entwined by mathematical equations and sacred geometry. The importance of Light needs no explanation for without it all would be darkness and because of the Light we are able to see. The second main function is the Light reflects off the Sound and produces images, in a similar way to a film, and appears, to our minds, to be solid. All life and all forms in existence are a combination of Sound and Light. This is the secret that scientists are desperate to find, but they never will because they are trying to find the invisible. The invisible creates magnetism and rotation, the two main functions of the universe. Quantum physics believes there must be some form of structure holding everything in place; the basis of this structure is Light and Sound, which I will discuss later.

Ah, look! Billy Sideways is coming down the lane. I bet he is making his way to Ann's Tea Room to scrounge a cup of tea and maybe a cake. I haven't seen him for quite some time. You don't see many tramps with characters nowadays. He's got one brown shoe and one black, and with that old raincoat and funny hat, he looks like a large version of Worzel Gummidge with his white beard and ragged clothes. He's had that old bike for years, and he pushes it around everywhere he goes, with all his possessions in those bags tied on the back. He can't ride it because he's taken the pedals off. Notice how his head is turned sideways but he's walking straight forwards – that's because he is so badly boss-eyed he has to turn his head sideways to look forwards. That's how he got the name Sideways. Mind you, everyone looks after him, giving him food and such. His coat is torn on the right sleeve and one pocket is missing. Two-planks gave him one of his old coats some years ago, and straight away he tore the sleeve and one of the pockets off. Must be his trademark.

About four years ago, he caused a car to crash into the river at Squealer's Corner. He was looking right at the time, but because his head was facing forward, the driver of the car thought he wasn't looking as he stepped out, so he swerved to miss him and went into the river. They had to call out the local garage to pull him out. Luckily, there was no damage. It looks as though they've taken him into the local hospital and given him a good clean up and trimmed his hair and beard. They do that every so often. There he goes up to Ann's Tea Room, just as I thought.

Why Light and Sound?

First, we must understand that the Dreamer has intelligence far greater than we can understand yet, at the same time, very simple, with a mathematical and geometrical basis.

First, sound was given the ability to be separated by varying degrees of pitch and volume. For example, music is an arrangement of sound consisting of different frequencies, i.e. notes, played at varying speeds and volumes, but most importantly, each sound has the ability to pass through itself without any distortion occurring. This is why you can hear all the individual notes and instruments in an orchestra. If we look at light, this also has been given the quality of variance in brilliance and colour, as in a rainbow, and, like sound, has the gift of passing through itself. This you may have seen in a laser light show. One other important quality is they can both be reflected without distortion, such as in an echo or moonlight reflecting off the sea. You must remember that in our human body, our range of hearing is very limited; for example, man cannot hear a dog whistle but a dog can. Now you can appreciate that the possible combinations of sound, with different notes and volumes, and light, of different colours and intensity, are endless, suggesting eternal possibilities of creation.

Ah... here come the sandwiches! Mmm, they smell delicious! The homemade bread is wonderfully soft and light and melts in the mouth!

Before we tuck into our sandwiches, I would like you to listen carefully because this may be the closest that we will come to understanding the Dreamer.

Everything in creation is vibrating to a particular note or notes and its corresponding colours. If we had the ability to listen to creation, we would more than likely hear beautiful melodies in varying pitch and volumes of HU and see a beautiful display of light in every changing degree of light and colour because creation is energy moving in rhythms and harmonies determined by magnetism.

These rhythms and harmonies were created by the Dreamer separating the Sound into a mathematical sequence consisting of seven notes. These notes are known as follows: do, re, mi, fa, sol, la and ti, ever rising or descending. There is no such thing as an octave in music; there are only seven notes. Also note that the Light is divided into seven colours, namely, red, orange, yellow, green, blue, indigo and violet. There are three primary colours, namely, red (positive), yellow (neutral) and blue (negative).

This Divine Melody is beauty in motion, and it is beauty that creates love. Now listen closely and try to understand this because if you can grasp this, then the rest of the teachings should fall into place more easily. The Dreamer is ever singing its melodies of HU according to Its dream, which we are part of, and this, in turn, creates love for the Dreamer. If the Dreamer stopped loving Its dream, then the music or HU would stop and there would be nothing. Therefore, we exist only because the Dreamer loves us. This is how the saying "God is Love" came about, but the Dreamer is beauty in motion, the Creator of Love, and the word "God" has another meaning.

Mmm! I love the taste of toast when it's burnt! My mum used to give me soot to eat; she said it was good for the blood, and if you had a boil, she would give you soot and butter to eat. We even cleaned our teeth with soot! This cheese has a unique taste. It's made by a small cheese factory about 20 miles north from here. It's got a sort of smoky taste.

I expect you are wondering why, if the Dreamer creates love and loves us, there is so much pain and destruction. First let me explain the Big Bang, which science keeps on about, because it leads to that question.

A WALK IN THE RAIN

Chapter 3

The Creation of Opposites

*W*e used to play skiffle on a Saturday night in the other bar. I was the washboard player, and my washboard consisted of two washboards joined together. I also had a pair of gloves with metal button sewn on the fingers. The bass was an old wooden tea chest with a broom handle standing on top and a string running from the centre of the chest to the top of the broom handle. The way to change the note was to pull the string tight by pulling the handle back for the higher notes. We had guitars and drums as well. That was the beginning of rock and roll. Then I went on to play the guitar, and I still have it in my loft. I did try singing but got fed up with being covered in tomatoes!

The creation of the universe is quite interesting, but first you must try to understand that in the home of the Dreamer, which is the Sea of Sound and Light, there is no time and space. The Sound and Light are not separated; neither are the positive and negative poles. This is also your home where you were created and given life. Our universe was NOT created by a big bang; this is an undisputable fact. The whole secret of creation lies in the shape of the Baby Universe, of which a picture was taken in February 2003.

The Light is electrically charged, and the Sound passes through the Light structure and becomes magnetic. Everything is controlled by magnetism.

It may be interesting for you to learn the four main qualities of Sound. These are Character, Rhythm, Magnetism and Substance. The protons, neutrons and electrons are given substance. Their own unique qualities and quantities relative to one another are determined by the character. Their orderly movement and life is brought about by the rhythm and it is the magnetism that determines the rhythm and how the atoms organise themselves into cells and into extremely complex organisms. I hope this has helped you see that creation is basically Sound and Light organised by magnetism into rhythmic components of the opposites, protons and electrons.

It is not necessary for me to go into more explicit detail, but there is one very important point that most people, whether they be scientific or spiritual in mind, have not considered: why create time and space by splitting the two poles, positive and negative? Now listen carefully because this is one of the most important aspects of life on Earth. By splitting these two poles, the Dreamer created OPPOSITES. It had no other choice. As soon as the Dreamer created, It created the opposite. If there was darkness, It created the opposite, which is the Light – Light and Dark. In the beginning was silence, and then the opposite, Sound, was created.

All life is governed by opposites. First there is life and death, man and woman, day and night, hot and cold; in fact, there is nothing that doesn't have its opposite. This has more significance than one can imagine, and its importance has been overlooked.

Shall we make a move? I'll just say goodbye to the barman – "Thanks, Ted – see you later." We'll turn right and – oh hang on, I've left my hat in the pub... We'll follow the public footpath just down the road by the tall hedge. The wind is a bit stronger down here because it whirls down the valley. Look at that piece of paper skipping down the road as though it is dancing with joy, then doing a pirouette every so often as it catches an eddy in the wind, stopping every now and then as if catching its breath before skipping off again. It's amazing the power the wind has, created by the opposites of hot and cold air.

One small point I would like to explain. There is life only in a physical form on Earth, and each life form, whether it be animal, vegetable or mineral, has to contend with the opposites, which is predator and prey. Disease and time are the two most potent predators, and nothing can escape time; even Earth will succumb to time. The only thing that is permanent on Earth is change. Now, one logical look at opposites before we move on. The Dreamer realised that each opposite must be equal to or as important as the other; therefore, one must pass through one to gain the other. Remember this well as it is the key to freedom. One **must** *pass through the darkness to reach the light, and one must pass through the silence to hear the sound. There is no other way.*

Here is the footpath which leads to Nowhere. As you can see, the old path is somewhat meandering. It must have been started by the old boys who walk home drunk from the Mudhole. You can just imagine the old boys walking home a bit tipsy, zig-zagging across the field, holding one another up, while their wives were waiting for them with the rolling pin! There are two old trees further up that are so entwined they look like two lovers embracing.

I would like you to believe and understand that life is indestructible and you are life. It is a particle of Sound and Light. It is what some call spirit, with the ability to be one with the whole or individualized. The best way to explain this is to take water, for example. You can turn water into a spray, but the droplets will immediately rejoin as one whole; therefore, it would be a good description to call spirit a Sea of Sound and Light. As I said, you are a speck of Sound and Light with the Dreamer's gift of consciousness and the ability to know, to see and to be. You are living in a world of opposites in time and space.

There are the two trees! It seems they are both competing for the same space. Even the branches are entwined, as if in a loving embrace. Some call them the love trees. As you can see, young lovers have carved their names in the trunks. Some say it will bring them luck in love. It is funny how people believe in things like that but have little time for the secrets of the Dreamer. Is my name on the trees? No, but it is in the old church, and I'll tell you why when we get there. You'll find it's a bit muddy further on, so we'll have to be careful.

A WALK IN THE RAIN

Chapter 4

Consciousness

*W*e'll take the left fork here; the other path goes up to Ann's Tea Room. We'll then cross the lane that leads to the old church and continue up the path to Nowhere. I can see the puzzled look on your face – Nowhere? It's the old tithe barn which belongs to Mr Richardson, who lives in the big house with the two round towers up there on the right We will see it better as we cross the lane. It looks rather haunted, with its dark grey stone wall and dull roof tiles. You can just imagine some eerie old butler opening that creaking, weather-beaten oak door, saying, "Come in," with a deep, slow, haunting voice. Even the eyes of the gargoyles on the parapet wall seem to watch you as you pass – see what I mean?

When I was small, the other kids and I used to run past the house because we thought two witches lived there. They were actually two old spinsters with pale, wrinkled faces peering out of that lower window on the right, one each side of a large aspidistra plant. Whenever you went by there, they were watching your every move with their beady eyes. When they died, Mr Richardson bought the house. That's the path at the end of the stone wall. It's like a tunnel from here on where the trees have grown over.

We are life, and the quality of life is consciousness. Although we are a consciousness, we need something to be conscious of. This is awareness. Imagine being born in a dark room. Although you were conscious, you wouldn't be aware of anything other than darkness, so what good would it be to you? Thus, the purpose of consciousness is to become aware. Here lies the purpose of life on Earth, and it consists of two main attributes. At this point, I am going to depart from the more traditional views, which are learning right from wrong or being responsible for yourself. The disadvantage of the traditional spiritual viewpoint is it makes us judge one another, making some believe they are better than others, but unbeknown to most, this viewpoint hides a more subtle objective for the consciousness and is all connected to the creation of opposites and the law that corresponds with it. Listen closely: there is neither right nor wrong, neither good nor bad; there is just what there is. Bear with me as you may not agree at the moment, but things are not what they seem.

It's rather dark in this tunnel of trees, but the birds seem to love it, especially the sparrows. They fly in here out of the hot sun in the summer and out of the wind in the winter. As you can hear, they make quite a racket with their chirping as though they were having a good natter. They seem to have got used to people walking past. Some sit on the branches watching you cheekily, tilting their heads sideways to get a better view.

Those who are under the impression that the Dreamer created evil are degrading the Dreamer and Its intelligence. In fact, the Dreamer only created opposites. As I have said before, It had no other option. This is important. Opposites were created so that the consciousness, or you, can become aware of those opposites by experiencing them through life on Earth and can compare those opposites. Now here's the crux of the matter. The purpose of comparisons is for you to have a preference. Preference is one quality for you to become aware of, whilst the second is becoming aware that you are the keeper of the Creative Gem. How you obtain these qualities is an important part of your life, which we will talk about soon.

On the right here is the beautiful yellow of the rape field, which has a rather strong smell now it's in full bloom. You'll find there's a break in the trees ahead, with a nice view of the old church across the fields. It was my job, as a young boy, to pump the church organ every Sunday morning and night for six old pence. I was originally in the boys' choir, but I used to pull faces at the girls and make them laugh, so I was made to pump the organ instead.

Mr Cooklyn was the vicar, and his wife used to play the organ. She was a rather large, stern woman, to say the least, with eyes that would look right through you. She had to turn sideways to squeeze between the church pew and the organ. They even reinforced the stool she sat on to play the organ. I used to sit just round the right-hand side of that organ, out of sight of the congregation, just behind the girls' choir. My job was to watch the gauge, which was a piece of pipe about 2 inches long on a piece of string. When you pumped, it used to go up to a mark showing when it was full of air, and down to a mark when it was empty. If it went below the bottom mark, the organ would run out of air and make strange noises. I often used to tell jokes to the girls and forgot to look at the gauge. When the organ ran out of air, Mrs Cooklyn would glare at me and whisper, "Pump, you fool!" One Sunday night, it ran out of air just as the choir stopped singing, but it was too late. She shouted, "Pump you fool!" and the whole church heard her. Boy, was she cross! I lost my six pence that night.

George and I spent quite a few years pumping away. George was the church mouse, and his hole was just under my chair. When he came out, he used to take one look at Mrs Cooklyn and his little legs would shake with fear before he scurried off behind the altar. I would bring some arrowroot biscuits, crushed up, for George, so we became used to one another! If you go in there, you will find my name carved on the side of the organ. You can't miss it — the letters are about nine inches high!

See that old bare tree which was struck by lightning a few years ago? It looks as though a large witch's hand, with long, disfigured fingers, is emerging from the ground. Especially at dusk, you can just imagine a vulture perched on the top!

Over there is Nowhere!

A WALK IN THE RAIN

Chapter 5

The Divine Gem

*W*hen we get to the end of the path, it gets quite steep, so it may be rather slippery. Luckily a handrail was fixed after Miss Richardson slipped one day in the mud; by the time she managed to stand up, it looked as though she'd been in a mud fight.

I suppose you are wondering what the Creative Gem is that we are keeping. Before I tell you, I would like to say that without it, there would be nothing, and man would never have been able to advance. The Gem is the spark of all life and the chief instigator of change and evolution.

Whoops! Nearly fell then! Good job I've got hold of the handrail! We used to race our bikes down here; it was a lot narrower then. I tried to ride with no hands and went through the hedge and stuck a branch through my leg. Still got the scar to remind me. In fact, I've got scars all over the place, ribs that stick out and other oddities that I've collected on the way. Phew, here we are at last at Nowhere. My boots weigh a ton with all this mud on them. I'll just sit on this old plough for a while. I suppose you're ok?

There are quite a few old bits of farming equipment left here, all from a bygone age. It is by using the Creative Gem that things have advanced. See how the brambles have slowly been creeping over, with their long green tentacles twisting their way round and round, ever tightening their choking grip, while the stinging nettles inch their way through the gaps, slowly devouring the past. That spider there is building its web from the handle of that old potato planter to the hawthorn bush. I often wondered how they get the web across from one side to the other. Look, he's just started going round. Did you know every other turn is laced with glue, so he has to remember which is which, otherwise he would get stuck himself! It looks as though it's made of rows of small diamonds as the light reflects off the droplets of rainwater. When he's finished, he'll shake the web to remove some of the droplets.

It is by using the Creative Gem that all life has managed to adapt to catching its prey or defending itself against its predators. Even bacteria and microscopic organisms use the Gem to try and overcome obstacles such as antibiotics. So what do you think this Creative Gem is? Most people seem to take it for granted, yet we never stop using it. Scientists are struggling to find the answer to life and the universe. The thing that they are trying so hard to find is the thing they are using to find it! So what is the Creative Gem? The Divine Creative Gem is IMAGINATION.

Imagination is the only reality that exists. It is the image maker, the creator of thought. It is the very heart of the Dreamer and is also at the heart of all life. It is the cause of all that is. Imagination needs no space, yet it contains all space and time and can expand with its creation for eternity. Now this is the irony of it. Science is searching for something that doesn't exist. It is a no thing, meaning it has no substance, yet it is everything; it is just a dream. Let me explain. When you dream, that dream appears to be real, with colour, sound, movement and light. When you stop dreaming, it disappears. If the Dreamer stopped dreaming, everything would just disappear! The question is why has It given you part of Its Creative Gem?

Listen very carefully and take note. You are part of the Dreamer, ever expanding. It has given you a part of Itself, Imagination, to learn how to create in a positive way by becoming aware of the correct preferences which you achieve by passing through the opposites. For without this Gem, you would not be able to function, to create thoughts or ideas.

Let's see how it works. Take man. He imagined going to the moon and this became his dream. He used his intelligence and slowly gained knowledge. With determination, he finally fulfilled his dream. Imagination is the creator. It is the faculty that gives you life. Therefore, you are the keeper of the Creative Gem.

Nice and peaceful up here! Even the old barn has an air of tranquility, with its aged timbers and twisted frame. The ivy and honeysuckle seem to embrace it as though protecting it against the weather; their gentle green leaves huddle together with a splash of colour to brighten the weary air of old age. There's something magical which time gives to old buildings, a sense of belonging.

The small wildflowers dotted on the ground make it look as if someone had walked by with a can of yellow and blue paint, dripping it as they went. It reminds me of a time when men were more contented with life because there was nothing to have, only one another's company.

Most people are not aware of the purpose of opposites and look upon negative situations as though they should not exist, yet that is how it's meant to be. There are those who care for the world and its people and wish to have peace and prosperity for all. Unfortunately, the world does not work that way. The law of opposites will not allow this, and there will always be wars and poverty to counterbalance peace and prosperity.

Oh! I forgot to tell you why this place is called Nowhere! Courting couples used to come up here in the summertime, and when they were asked where they had been, they would say, "Nowhere!" The name became more of a joke and then it became permanent.

A WALK IN THE RAIN

Chapter 6

The Percentage of the Opposites

*W*hile we are having a rest in this delightful spot, I would like to explain about the percentage of the opposites.

If you look back in time, you will find that each country rises to its highest point of influence and power in the world either by might or by financial wealth, technology and the arts and then declines. For instance, the Aztecs, the Egyptians, the Greeks, the Romans, Great Britain and the United States of America. These golden years, as they are called, are brought about by the percentage of the opposites' wealth or poverty, and it is not by accident but by design that these opposites are controlled in accordance with the Dream.

Each country has its exact position in the world ranking. For example, after the Second World War, a struggle developed between the two opposites of East and West. One side became powerful in military might, with its weapons and armed men, while the other side became powerful in wealth and technology but had less might. At the point of approximate equilibrium, the might was dismantled by one man, and the wall separating the two was demolished. This left an imbalance of opposites: one side was left with less might and no wealth, whilst the other side had wealth and might. Consequently, you have, on one side, a high percentage of poverty, and on the other, you have a high percentage of wealth. The dismantling was in accordance with the Master of the Dream. You will find that the country which is at the bottom of influence has a very high percentage of poverty. As you can see, the opposites have far more influence over our lives than people could ever imagine. One thing you should remember is that there are no winners or losers. It only appears that way. Everything is in its right place at the right time.

Oh, it's almost stopped raining! I hadn't noticed. Here comes Raymond with his golfing umbrella, walking his dog, Nipper.

"Hi, Raymond! I see you are braving the weather?"

"Yes, it's miserable, but if I don't take Nipper out, he sits and barks until I do."

"How's the wife? I heard she twisted her ankle?"

"Almost better, thanks. She slipped getting off the bus two weeks ago."

"If you are going down Richardson's way, you will find it's a bit slippery at the start. We don't want you twisting your ankle as well!"

"Thanks."

"Bye, Raymond."

He doesn't like to be called Ray, you know. A bit snooty in his younger days – always had to call him Raymond, otherwise he wouldn't answer. Ha ha, I gave him a black eye at school because he wouldn't let me play table tennis. It was a month before he spoke to me again. I'm surprised he never called his dog Charles. They called him Nipper because he used to nip your ankles when he was a puppy. They used to ask him if he'd fed Nipper with too much crab, which got up his nose somewhat. Mind you, he will always help you if you need it. His wife bought the dog off Mrs Clark. Apparently it was the runt of the litter, but he thinks a lot of him and they are always together. Some people get closer to their pets than to other people.

We'll head down this way by the tree struck by lightning a few years ago. Notice the strange sounds you get with the dripping of water off the trees. It can be quite eerie sometimes, as though someone is secretly following you! We'll go through Fairy Wood, which is quite a quaint place. It used to be a stone quarry many years ago but is now overgrown. You'll see why it's called Fairy Wood when we get there.

Do you remember playing with a magnet? Did you know that you were using the power of the Dreamer? Magnetism is the power of the opposites positive and negative, but the unique quality is that it can attract or repel, and by using these two opposites, one has the ability to suspend an object in space.

Each planet is held in place by magnetism. Now this is important for you to remember. All events are governed by controlling the opposites through magnetism. We can chat about this later, but if you remember magnetism is a quality of the Sound, it is therefore possible to charge each note with either positive or negative influences.

The path turns sharply to the left then sweeps round to the right. You'll see some lovely rhododendrons as we round the corner. There used to be a house there, something to do with the quarry, but it burnt down before the war, so it was bulldozed flat and is part of the Richardson farm. Look, there's a sparrow hawk over to your right. Stand still! He's spotted something in the hedgerow. It's amazing how his head stays perfectly still while the rest of his body is compensating for the wind and his wing movements. It is as though someone has glued his head in that position and the rest of his body is trying to escape. He's dived and got something. I can't see; it could be a field mouse.

It may be time to talk about the Master of the Dream, but before I explain, there is also an opposite, and that is the Master of the Maze. That's made you frown! You may not believe it yet, but we are in the labyrinth of time, experiencing the effects of the Opposites.

Look, the rhododendrons are over there.

A WALK IN THE RAIN

Chapter 7

The Master of the Dream and its Opposite

*T*here! What do you think of those rhododendrons? The raindrops on the petals are creating a shimmering wall of dark and light mauve, with a dash of olive green as the wind shakes them as if trying to wake them from a dream. The ground beneath is like an eiderdown where the blossoms have drifted down and kissed the earth before settling down to sleep.

Now, can you see how beauty creates love? Have you got the feeling you would like to stay here forever? That's the feeling you have when you reach the Dreamer. Love is a feeling which comes from within, and what you find beautiful will stimulate this feeling. Let's go back to talking about the Master of the Dream and the Master of the Maze. If you can remember, I said that the percentage of the opposites is controlled. In fact, the whole universe, including our Earth, is under the guidance of a hierarchy. Some have immense power that is beyond man's understanding. These great beings do have names, but I have purposely eliminated any form of names whilst we are discussing such things. The reason for this is that man has a habit of creating rivalry between different names which actually describe the same thing; some think theirs is superior and the others a farce, but all they have done is created opposites, superior and inferior.

The hierarchy of the Dreamer consists of first the Dreamer, the Lord of All. Next we have the Master of the Dream, and then we have the Nine Unknown Ones. They are the guardians of the Nine, which is the secret code of creation and the code of opposites and its corresponding law that governs our lives. The whole of creation is based on mathematical codes connected to sacred geometry, but that is another story.

To assist the Master of the Dream, we have the Dream Masters. The last I will mention are the Workers of the Dream. The opposite of these are the Master of the Maze and Its subordinates, who are grouped into brotherhoods of varying colours. The rest are Workers of the Maze.

The purpose of the hierarchy of the Maze is to keep you in the Maze and guide you through so that you experience all the combinations of the opposites. This includes passing through all the races of man, with their customs, and experiencing male and female and all the positions of power and rejection. The time span is in four sections, rather like the four seasons in a year, so we can call them the four seasons of time. It is the transition of opposites running from positive to negative. The first season is the positive end of the scales where man experiences mainly the five virtues of life, which are Forgiveness, Chastity, Humility, Detachment and Contentment. This is known as the Golden Age.

The second season is the introduction of the negative opposites of the virtues, which are the five passions of Lust, Anger, Attachment, Vanity and Greed. This is where man starts to quarrel, and this season is known as the Silver Age. The third season is where the negative passions outweigh the positive virtues. This season heralds the introduction of wars and turmoil and is known as the Bronze Age. Last is the fourth season where the negative passions dominate man's life, and we are starting to enter this stage now. It is this stage of man's journey which is most important, as you will discover, and it's all in accordance with the Dream.

That double row of oak trees used to be the driveway to the house. As you can imagine, it must have been quite impressive, but now the cows appreciate them for their shade in the summer. We're now coming up to Fairy Wood. Notice these large boulders scattered around like seats for some giants to sit upon. There is a lovely smell in the air coming from those yellow azaleas. It's amazing the different fragrances flowers produce, all competing for the attention of the bees to pollinate their species.

We will have to be careful in Fairy Wood because the path follows a winding course down into the quarry and up the other side. Everything seems fresh in the spring, with an air of newness. See these big boulders, some standing on others as though someone had knocked down an old castle many years ago. The moss has covered them, giving them the appearance of being made of green velvet. Strange, eerie fingers hold them in place, the roots of the trees leaning at peculiar angles as they sprout out of obscure cracks in the rocks. The path seems to split in two directions but then meets up again just round the other side of the boulders. Mind the steps as we climb down in an ever-twisting descent, passing through narrow passageways. Look out for the surprise, and it's not the dripping creepers that slap you in the face as you round each corner! Ha ha! I see you've found it! Catches you by surprise! A giant glass eye with a penetrating stare imbedded in the rock, which makes you shudder! No one knows who put it there. It just appeared one day, but it became the talk of the village for quite some time. Parents tell their children it is the "All-Seeing Eye" which can see them even when they are at school and in bed.

We are nearly at the bottom – just a few more twists. There! What do you think of that pool of lime green water? It's quite unique. Something to do with the chemicals in the rocks. You can just imagine a friendly green dragon popping its head out and asking, "Have you come to see the wizard?" There are some more surprises on the other side as we climb out. Shall we rest here for a while? Have you noticed the echo in here? Hello...hello...hello..."

A WALK IN THE RAIN

Chapter 8

Where we come from and where we go

Quite magical sitting here with the green velvet boulders towering above our heads and the overhanging branches giving the appearance of unfinished umbrellas. The birds are singing, producing strange repeating sounds because of the echoes. You have this odd feeling that there are lots of eyes watching you, but it's more in a friendly way than spooky

No doubt you have been wondering where the real us has come from. First you must realise that the Dreamer is forever creating and expanding Its Dream, so it is obvious It needs to fill Its dream with workers of the dream to maintain and run it. This is accomplished by creating individual atoms of consciousness with the gift of the Gem, Imagination. Consciousness is conceived in the Realms of Pure Sound and Light in a cocoon-shaped structure consisting of honeycomb compartments, similar to a bee's nursery. No other than the Dreamer can create consciousness. It is the Father and Lord of All. When the consciousness is fully formed, it is given an identity that is called Soul. Firstly, you must understand that you are soul. It is not a part of you, it is YOU. When the time is right, as a new soul, it will be transported through one of seven exits, each exit having its colour ray and sound. When you pass through this exit, it is then that you descend into the Maze of Opposites, which exists in time and space.

The descent into the physical world on Earth requires soul to pass through five descending worlds of consciousness, each one having a unique function to make up the human being.

Look, I will explain these descending worlds by drawing them in the gravel path. If I draw a line at the top, this is the Dreamers World, and under this is the beginning of the Maze.

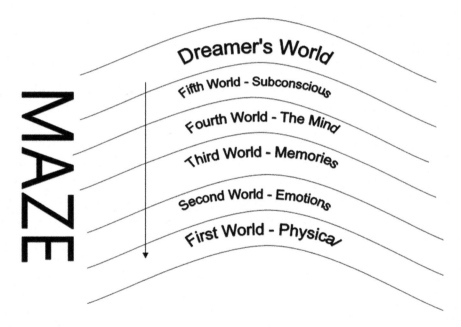

The Fifth World is the higher part of the Mind, the subconscious and intuition. Under this is the Fourth World, which is the Mind. Under this we have the Third World, which is concerned with memories. Next we descend into the Second World, which is concerned with emotions. Lastly we have the physical world.

These worlds are described as descending because the vibration rate is lower for each world as it passes through them. Here, you will see I have drawn a curvedline alongside each world representing the vibration of that world and you will see that as we descend, the vibration gets larger, representing a lower frequency. This means, quite simply, that the atomic structure is vibrating at a lower vibration than the world above it. As soul passes through these worlds, it requires a body to cover soul so that it can function on that level.

Let me explain why soul needs these bodies. I'm sure you are aware that a glass can be broken by a high-pitched note. In fact, any obstacle in the physical world can be distorted by a high enough frequency. Now soul is at the opposite end to the physical body, and its frequency is extremely high, so if soul came into the physical world, it would be unable to cope with the heavier vibrations of that world. If you put the glass into a box, the high note would not break it. Equally, soul needs to be put in a box, hence a body. As soul descends, it needs another body that will allow it to operate in each particular world. This will help you understand how complex a human being you are. If you realise that you function on five levels of consciousness and you also have five layers of bodies, which also correspond to the five worlds of different frequencies, it will help you understand yourself much better.

If you can imagine these descending frequencies are like different radio waves, each station is passing through the atmosphere but can only be heard by tuning into that frequency, such as Radio 1 or Radio 2. You may be able to see why the Dreamer created the Sound and Light with the ability to pass through themselves without distortion.

Now, for the unique functions of the five levels of consciousness, I will keep this as simple as possible. First is our physical body, which is constructed of muscle and bone and so on. This is controlled mainly by the second emotional body, by the five passions of Lust, Anger, Attachment, Vanity and Greed. Second is the emotional body which holds and distributes your emotional feelings. Third is the memories or record of past events, which is like a library. Fourth is the mind, which sorts out our likes and dislikes, and fifth is the intuition and subconscious body, which holds our fears and intuition. Put all these together and we have what you believe is you, but you are operating these as soul.

Shall we make a move? It is a bit of a climb, but you will see why it is called Fairy Woods. It gets rather narrow just round the corner and low with the overhanging branches, so we will have to duck down. It is like a cave where some large boulder is resting on top of others. Aaagh! A bird flew out of a crack – gave me quite a jump! When we get out of this tunnel, look over to the right. Mind this wet creeper hanging down. Oooh! That's better, I can straighten my back. So, over to the right, you can see a ring of twelve stones, each one carved to look like a fairy. They call it the Fairy Ring, and it's always got invisible fairies dancing in the middle – so they say! Children are told if they can see an invisible fairy, they can have a wish come true. In the summer when the parents bring their children, you can see them all looking for quite some time. Some children even say they can see a fairy; it keeps them occupied for hours.

When we get to the top, you can see Ann's Tea Room. How about a cup of tea and some home-made cakes? Sound good? OK! The trees are smaller here because the soil is very shallow and the moss even grows on the trees, making them look furry to match the rocks. There, we are at the top, and here you can see how nature has provided us with magic of its own – a carpet of enchanting bluebells. Come over this way; that's Ann's Tea Room. It used to be the old blacksmith's shop. On the way to Ann's, there is a row of pink horse chestnuts or conker trees. I have never known the difference between the white and the pink, but we reckoned that the pink trees produced the hardiest conkers! It is nice to see the boys still play conkers! While we amble down to Ann's, I will tell you about the Maze.

43

A WALK IN THE RAIN

Chapter 9

Level of Consciousness

*W*hen we enter the Maze of Opposites in time and space, we pass through our given colour archway. We pick up our coverings on each of the five levels as we descend to the physical world of Earth. We then enter the first stage of our evolution, which is in the mineral kingdom, and this, as you can imagine, is very limited. At this stage, we are not an individualised soul but what is known as a group soul. This means, quite simply, that soul is in control of a mass of minerals.

After a given period of time, we will progress to the next stage of our evolution in the vegetable kingdom, gaining a higher level of awareness and still as a group soul, but this has diminished in size. For instance, it could be controlling a forest of trees or many acres of grass.

After passing through all the vegetable states of awareness, we come into the animal kingdom. As we progress through the animal kingdom, the group soul gradually diminishes in size. For example, the group soul may be in control of a family of ants, then after some time, it is in control of a herd of buffaloes, then a pride of lions and finally, just two animals. At this point, it is time for us to become individualised and become a Human Being.

If we look at the name Human Being, it is not by accident because its meaning is quite clear. "Hu", as I have said, is the Sound and Light or Spirit. "Man" means individual and "Being" means consciousness. Therefore Hu-man-being means spirit's individual consciousness. This is where we, as soul, have the opportunity to really achieve progress in the use of our Creative Gem, Imagination, and experience the huge combination of opposites to gather our preferences.

Listen! A cuckoo! Shh! It's over there in that maple tree. I haven't heard one for a few years. My mum used to say the cuckoo's come out to dry the mud up. If ever a bird used its Creative Gem, it was the cuckoo, laying its egg in some other bird's nest, then going off to play, as you would say. There must be quite a few parents who would like to do that. Also, people today are ever desiring more material goods than they really need, which, in turn, creates more stress for themselves, but what have they gained? Nothing! Perhaps they have gained more envy or jealousy, but very rarely contentment. Find contentment and you've found peace.

You may be wondering why we don't come straight into the human consciousness. Let's look at it as though we were the Dreamer. The Earth needs mineral, vegetable and animal components to function for man to have a livable planet. The body needs minerals to function, as well as vegetables and meat. Therefore, it is obvious that one must start at the bottom of the ladder; otherwise, the others would not be able to progress to become Hu-manized. As you can see, it is logical and could be no other way.

That's Ann's place – see the crooked chimney. It was built that way to stop the downdraft blowing the smoke into the place. As I said, it was the blacksmith's workshop belonging to Wally Lovell. He was rather a short, stocky chap with dark, sparkling eyes. His skin was like leather where the heat of the forge had dried it like a prune! He was always whistling a one-note tune, and it sounded as though one front tooth was missing. He had a funny habit of rubbing his right cheek with the back of his hand whilst talking to you, and because he never shaved in the morning, it made a scratching sound on his stubble, like rubbing sandpaper over his cheeks. He made the wrought iron gates for the Richardsons' house. Had a way with horses; he looked them in the eye and they were sort of hypnotised. He was well-liked by everybody, especially us when we were kids. When he retired, Ann got permission to turn the building into a tea room.

Wally used to make us sledges for the winter snow, every one different with a name on the side and a badge on the front. Mine was called Mountain Storm. Brian Hall's was called the Downhill Devil; Mickey Carson's I think was called Snow Crusher. Everyone loved old Wally. He was happy working in his shop, contented just to be what he was. When he left the body, you couldn't get into the church for his funeral service because people came from miles away. He must have had a happy life to be loved by so many.

Before we get to Ann's, I would like to explain that all human consciousness and animals cared for by humans are joined together by circumstances and events which are by design. For example, you have your circle of friends, family and maybe workmates. Each one of those has connections with others you do not know and so it goes on and on. If you investigated, you would find it would extend all round the world. Therefore, we are all part of the Maze through circumstances and events. Now, the secret is to become detached from the influences and events of others, which is not an easy task.

Here we are! See the sign on the wall in wrought iron: "Wally's Workshop". Ann decided to leave it there to keep his memory alive. You will see some photos of Wally inside. In you go.

A WALK IN THE RAIN

Chapter 10

The Workings of the Maze

Get out, you fool! Get out!"

"No, it's ok; it is only Morris the mynah bird! Shut up, Morris."

"Hi, Ann! I see Morris is up to his old tricks!"

"Yes, he'll have to go out the back."

"Out the back, out the back," repeats Morris "Shut up, Morris. You are noisy this afternoon! I'll cover him up; that normally quietens him down. What are you doing out in this weather?"

"We came out for a walk, so we've popped in for tea and cake. Was Sideways here this morning?"

"Yes. He hasn't been around for some time. I gave him some food and drink, then off he went, pushing his bike towards Oakford."

We'll sit in the corner. Shh! I'll let you in to a secret! When Ann brought the mynah bird and called him Morris, we thought it was funny because the name reminded me of the car Morris Minor! So me and Ted, who was the barman in the Mudhole, put an ad in the county paper saying Morris Minor for Sale (spelling mynah as in minor), excellent condition, only £200 pounds. As you can imagine, poor Ann was inundated with phone calls inquiring about the Morris Minor. Apparently, one chap drove 50 miles to come and have a look at it. He was furious when he found it was a mynah called Morris. If Ann found out it was me and Ted, I would think she would be quite cross. "I'll have a pot of tea and two slices of coffee and walnut cake, please, Ann. That bread pudding looks good; you decide what you would like.

Before I tell you about this tea room, I think you should understand how the Maze works. I hope you understand about the five levels of consciousness. It is important to understand the workings of the Maze in time and space. First let us look at time. I will try to make it as simple as possible. As you are aware, time is a one-way progression, meaning that we can only go forwards in time and never backwards. We are all travelling through time, which is a continuous flow of, let's say, seconds so you can relate to time more easily. Once you have created some form of action, whether it is just a thought action or physical action towards some other life form, it cannot be undone, whether you regret it or are pleased with it. What's done is done. Your action is now locked in time. You must understand that our actions in time are always being recorded by the Lords of Time, as in a giant logbook of events. The real name for these I do not know, but they are kept on the third level of descent. If you can remember, I said that the third level of descent was the Record of Past Events, which is like a library. Now things are starting to fit together.

Ah! Here are the tea and cakes.

"Thanks, Ann, I've been looking forward to this."

Quite an interesting place, this. As you can see, Ann's left it in its original state. She wanted it as though Wally was still working here. She had all his tools and the old forge coated with a special lacquer so she could keep them clean without destroying their used look. I can still see Wally banging away on the red-hot iron work in the summer when he had all the doors and windows open. You could hear his hammer ringing on the anvil across the fields while a plume of smoke rose gently from the chimney, and if the summer breeze was in the right direction, you could just make out his one-note whistle.

Now listen, this is important and also complex. Are you concentrating? The Maze is full of events in a series of seconds or moments, ever flowing by the law of action and reaction, which appears as time to the mind. This law is the Law of Opposites, and this law states everything returns to its origin. According to the Law of Opposites, once you have acted or reacted, the course is set and locked in time. This also locks in time the opposite direction. What this means is quite simple. What goes out from you must come back. The Law of Opposites is the going and the coming. I will explain this in detail soon, but first of all, life is a combination of action and reaction connected like a gigantic web on all five levels of consciousness. All events in time are pre-ordained, according to your records, under the guidance of the Lords of Time, working through either one or several of the descending levels of consciousness but mainly through the second Emotional level. Not until you have experienced the coming back of your action has the circle of opposites been completed and that series of events can be concluded.

None can escape the Law of Opposites. I can see the look of horror on your face. Go on, say it! What about free will if all events are preordained? A wise man once said, "Free will? Of course you have free will; you have no choice!" That answer is the truth. It is for you to understand. No one can give you understanding, only you yourself by becoming aware.

If you look up over the old forge, you will see that the timbers are scorched because Wally only had a tin chimney at first. When it went rusty, instead of the heat going out of the chimney, it came out through the holes and scorched the timbers. That's when they built the brick chimney, and the builders built a double corbel, making it look crooked, but it worked very well. Fancy another pot of tea?

"Ann, another pot, please."

A WALK IN THE RAIN

Chapter 11

Free Will

*L*et me try to explain the Law of Opposites, which runs in circles. These *circles are attached not only to people but to nations and the whole world. First, let's see how the circle works and why it is in circles.*

Time and opposites are ever flowing forward in the form of a tunnel. If you imagine drilling a large hole in a wall, the drill is ever circling while moving forward, creating a hole. This is similar to our universe ever spinning whilst travelling outwards. You are like the tip of the drill experiencing the Now, the past is the hole you have just made with your actions, and the future is where you are going. Have I explained this well enough for you?

This is how it works. The circle is separated into four main sections, in the following order: going from you A through B, receiving by the opposite party C, then as it turns, the opposite comes into play, going from C (the other party) through D, and receiving by you A. Here, I will draw it on my napkin.

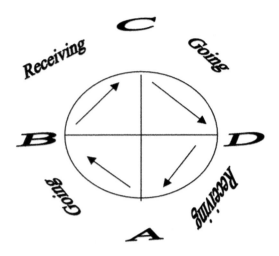

The whole world is covered in these circles with their corresponding set of notes, rhythms and harmonies. If one was able to see them, one would see trillions of circles, some connected to countries, others to large groups of people, small groups, families or individuals. Now, here is the important part, so concentrate. Some of these circles are completed, some are on the point of being completed and some will be completed in the future. Regarding the opposites of those circles, some have been created, some are just about to be created and some will be created in the future. Have you got that? These are the flowing events of action and re-action of time. This is the Maze, and the only way out is to complete all your circles of opposites.

Some people call this process karma, which states, "As you sow, so shall you reap." However, this statement causes fear in some people and they become frightened to do anything wrong in case they get it back. Everything is tied to the Law of Opposites. This law even governs the Dreamer Itself, and, as I have said, everything must return to its origin, including you and the Sound and Light. We must return to the Dreamer. Understand this: you can only return to the

Dreamer when all your actions have returned to their origin. All you will have is perfect preferences.

Note the difference between the concept of karma and the law of opposites. Firstly, you do not sow or reap anything. You must pass through all the opposites, and you are given these experiences in accordance with the Master of the Maze and his Lords of Time. So let's look at this in detail.

Each action, whether it be physical or just a thought, uses energy. This energy, which is part of you, is electromagnetic. When this energy is used, it is given off in a specific code according to your action. Just as an example, let's imagine you hate someone and you smash a window of his house. The action and the hate give off an energy code. Now, can you see you have used up the energy according to this code, and by the law of opposites, everything must return to its origin? This same amount of energy, with the same code and circumstances, must come back to be replaced. This applies to positive actions as well.

You may be wondering about the codes, what they are or where they go. If you remember, the third level of descent is where all records of events are stored. All codes of our actions are stored in your third body and can be read by the Lords of Time, who adjust each life accordingly.

The purpose of your having to experience the opposite of your action and reaction is so you have a comparison between the giving and the receiving of the bad passions or the good passions. Without comparisons, you would be unable to have preferences. There is no form of punishment, as many believe; the Dreamer would not contemplate such action.

If you killed someone's father out of anger and by your action the family had to sell their home and ended up very poor, by the law of opposites, the circle must be completed, as I have just explained. You would enter the tunnel of time and experience the role in reverse. Not only would you be killed by anger; you would also have to experience all the hardship you originally created for the family. Now you can compare the consequences of your action or reaction.

I suppose we should make a move. It's so cosy here, it's hard to get up and go outside.

"How much do I owe you, Ann? I've only got a twenty pound note. Thanks, Ann. Bye."

Are we ready?

It's amazing how some birds like Morris can imitate people's voices so accurately. They must be very aware of sound. It reminds me of the time when I was delivering some green groceries and I knocked on the door of a client's house. A voice said, "Come in!" so I went inside but there was no one in. "Hello," I said. "Hello," came the reply, and then I saw it was a parrot in the kitchen. The lady was out in the garden. She was quite shocked to find me in the house, but I explained the parrot had invited me in and she thought it was quite funny.

"Bye, Ann. Bye, Morris."

"**Hello! Come in**!" replied Morris from the back room.

A WALK IN THE RAIN

Chapter 12

Speed of Light

Quite a character, Morris. We'll be coming to the main road later. Mind this puddle – it's right across the track, so we ought to keep to the side. You never know how deep they are. That reminds me of the new policeman who came to the village when I was in my early twenties. He was a thin man with a narrow mouth, boney cheeks and deep-set eyes. When he told you off for something, there seemed to be a smirk on his face.

There was a gang of us who had cars. Mine was a blue Austin A35, Frank Rumsey had a white Ford Special which he built with a fiberglass body and Tim Norris had a Mini. Then there was Gannet; his real name was Dave Smith, but he always had a pocket full of sugar lumps to eat. He had a Mini with twin carburetors. Pete Harris had a Morris Minor van. We used to race home Saturday and Sunday nights from Medfield, which is about 20 miles away. We used to meet up with some other lads in the Old

House at Home, a rather delightful pub. Although I was a teetotaler, we used to have some fun there.

As you may guess, there weren't many cars about in those days, and there were no speed limits, only in the built up areas. When the new policeman, Constable Blake, arrived, he thought he was the Sheriff. The slightest thing wrong and he would pounce. Nobody liked him. He used to park his car in the entrance to one of Mr Watson's fields behind some trees just inside the 30 miles an hour limit coming into the village so he could catch you speeding. One Friday night, we dug a trench about a foot deep right across the field entrance where he parked. Mr Watson even gave us a hand! Then we covered it with a tarpaulin, pulling it tight with some thin pieces of wood across to stop it from sagging. We then sprinkled some dirt and leaves over. Yes, you've guessed it, Sheriff Blake backed into the pit! When the word got round, everybody drove past blowing their hooters. It was great! Of course, there was a great stink about it, but nobody knew anything. Sheriff Blake was moved away about a year later, and he was replaced by P.C. Harrigate, a nice old chap who fitted in well.

Are you still thinking about the Maze which is in the circles of time and opposites? This may help you understand. Some circles are completed very quickly, whilst others may take years or even centuries. Each circle spins at a different rate. Think of the workings of a clock, each wheel turning at a different rate but all interconnecting. Now imagine every person is in circles with other people's circles; it is mind boggling. Life is only a ride through time, whether it be long or short according to your circle. Your body is the vehicle, your feelings guide the direction, and the Creative Gem is used to create your Dream and your actions. This does not always work out; therefore, you need a flexible Gem.

You need to understand that the Maze can be entered in the past or the future, according to the experiences you need to have and what circles are being completed or started. If we could travel faster than light, we would then see the past. If we travelled at the speed of light, everything would stand still. Let me explain. Most of the stars we can see are not there anymore. They have moved on. Because the light has taken so long to reach us, we only see them where they were thousands of years ago. Therefore, we are looking at the past. Time is therefore relevant to light.

Let's make sure about this because it is so important that you understand. The light from the sun takes about 8 minutes to reach Earth. If you were half way to the sun, the light would take only 4 minutes. Now concentrate. If there was a huge explosion on the sun, it would take 4 minutes before you saw it, but 8 minutes before people on Earth saw it. Imagine once you had seen this explosion, you managed to get back to Earth in 3 minutes, you would see the same explosion in one minute's time on Earth. If you told people on Earth that you had already seen it, they would think you were mad, but you had seen the past of the sun by 4 minutes and the future of the Earth by 4 minutes.

When you enter time, you are only seeing a light image. If you enter at the time of the Battle of Hastings, it would appear to be real and you would go forward in time exactly as the light image was created, similar to the explosion on the sun. Remember, everything is Sound and Light. The Light reflects off the Sound, making images appear to be real, but it is only a dream. Everything appears solid and real because you are vibrating at the same rate of sound and light here in this physical world. Don't worry, you will get it!

At the end of the track are two walnut trees, which are rather old. We used to collect the walnuts years ago, and the outer coverings make your hands go brown and you can't get the stain off. My mum said walnuts grew on walls. It was quite some time before I saw them on the trees and realized she was joking!

Here we are on the main road. We'll turn right and walk up the road past these bungalows and then turn left at the Three Oaks. That footpath on the left goes down to the Mudhole where we saw Billy Sideways. These bungalows are rather nice. The bricks are of a rustic brown colour, and the large bay windows make them look spacious. The tall trees in their gardens give them nice shade in the summer. From their back gardens, they've got a lovely view across the valley, which was dammed in 1968, then flooded for the water company as a reservoir. It was nicely landscaped, as you will see, because we will be going that way. There was quite a lot of opposition to the reservoir, but now all the trees have grown and it is open to the public, so it's more like a park and the residents are pleased. There's the Three Oaks.

A WALK IN THE RAIN

Chapter 13

The Purpose of it All

*L*ovely oaks, these, with their broad trunks and large, sprawling branches as though they were trying to stretch themselves after emerging from the depths of the Earth. We don't know how old they are, but most of this area was woodland and was used for hunting by the gentry in the distant past. The common man just managed to scrape a living, while the gentry lived lavish lives, with no concern for the poor. This continues today in some parts of the world, just another cycle spinning its way around this globe as the percentage of the opposites changes the destiny of each country.

Now, what do you think of reincarnation? It's hard for most people to accept because they first need the knowledge we have discussed along the way. If you look at life as being just once, then life is unfair, with some people having really good lives and others having terrible lives. This would suggest it is a matter of pot luck. But let's look at this logically. Can you imagine the creation of the human form, with its complex DNA structure and the functions of man's brain, with its memory, complicated visual system, hearing mechanism, sense of feeling and so on, and how senseless it would be for it to pass through life in a haphazard way? Take a look at the machinery which you, as soul, are operating. The human being is a wonderful vehicle taking soul through a pre-ordained ride through time and then discarded at the end of each period of time. Once you understand that you, as soul consciousness, can leave the body and return in a different time in a different body, experiencing different opposites, your view on life will change dramatically for the better.

Why don't we remember other lives? There is a special reason why you do not remember past lives. Imagine having a life with a good body, lots of wealth and plenty of leisure; by the law of opposites, you would have to experience a life with an imperfect body, poverty and misery. If you could remember the really good life, it would be almost unbearable and may lead to suicide.

I would like to get you over the biggest hurdle, which is understanding and believing in reincarnation. Do you ever dream? Where do you think the light comes from to lighten your dream? If there were no light, it would be dark. Are you thinking? Now, one more thing. Who is watching the dream while you are asleep and your eyes are shut? Now listen! You have your own light. It is part of you, and you, as consciousness, can see, know and be. As I explained at the beginning, it was the REAL YOU watching the Dream.

Let's go back to the example I gave you about experiencing the opposite half of the circle of one's action. Imagine when, after killing the father, you had reached the point where you lost your house and life was really hard; then someone, out of compassion, had helped you to get back on your feet. You would then understand what is like to receive compassion and help, and you would have a comparison between creating misery and creating happiness. Do you see how all life is only leading to comparison then preferences? This is where the third level of descent comes in — memories of past events and past lives.

Although, consciously, you do not remember past events and lives, the effects are in your subconscious, which is the first vehicle. See how all five levels of consciousness work together? The more opposites you experience, the more preferences you bring into your life. Slowly, you become more in tune with the five positive preferences which are, if you remember, Forgiveness, Chastity, Contentment, Detachment and Humility.

The function of the Master of the Maze is to keep testing you to make sure your preferences are strong. When you reach a certain level of the correct preferences, it is time to come in contact with the Master of the Dream. Why is this important? If you remember, I said that only the Master of the Dream can get you out of the Maze. The Master of the Maze is always trying to keep you in the Maze with the five passions of the mind, Lust, Anger, Greed, Vanity and Detachment. When the Master of the Dream assesses you and finds you are ready, you will be led by him to the teachings of Sound and Light, and it is the Master that brings you to the point of perfect preference.

Lastly, as you progress, your use of the Creative Gem changes from negative creative action to positive creative action, which is the quality of the Dreamer. You are now qualified to learn to become a Worker of the Dream.

Turn left into that driveway. Those are lovely pansies there amongst the dwarf evergreens. We'll have to stop at the lodge house and get a number from God Bless. They close the area one hour before sunset, so they check the numbers back out to make sure no one is left inside overnight. If we follow the path to the left, we will be able to see the reservoir. There may be some wind surfers out today. They also have a sailing club and fishing. There! Not too bad coming up, was it? See what I mean by a lovely view? Although the reservoir is not very wide, it's quite long and, as you can see, it winds like a snake. They chose to flood this part of the river because it is a steep valley made by more of a gully than a hill each side. We'll sit on this bench for a few minutes and enjoy the view. It's time to tell you what happens once we leave this world. This should help you lose the fear of death and understand reincarnation.

A WALK IN THE RAIN

Chapter 14

Water Skiing

*A*re you enjoying the walk and discussion so far? The rain is not too bad, and once you get your mind occupied, you don't notice it. Regarding the discussion of life, it is more important to enjoy it rather than understand it because interest attracts attention, attention attracts knowledge and knowledge brings about understanding. Therefore, you should have some understanding by now of how and why the Earth and physical world were created. If you think you've got the gist of it, that's fine. It may be time to explain the process of death.

Firstly, the word death is not only horrible but inappropriate for what actually takes place because death means the end of existence and this is certainly not the case. The correct term is transmigration. If this term was widely used, it would relieve some of the fear that death instills in people. The timing of death – transmigration – is precise timing, not a minute before or a minute after the appropriate time but in accordance with the circle of time you are in. Remember this because it is important.

When the time comes to leave this world, at the point of transmigration, one just slips out of one's physical body. You will find yourself in a world of light which is brighter than on Earth and has a bluish tint. The body you are now in is the second one and is much finer in structure. Its atoms spin, which causes the light to reflect off them, resembling star dust. This is why it is called the Body of Light. This body has no bone structure, flesh or muscle because it is a spiritual body and not a physical one. It feels no pain and does not age. Most people assume they are in heaven, but alas, they are not. It is a place of rest before returning to Earth in a different body with different circles of opposites to contend with. This return to Earth is also exactly timed in accordance with the circles of time which determine the family, the country and the environment you will live in; in other words, all the circumstances of your life. This may be hard to accept, but it is so.

It is hard to relate to a body without bones and muscles, but it is only in this physical world that they are needed. The coverings or bodies we receive on the other four levels of worlds which we pass through whilst descending are similar to the Body of Light, but each one is finer in substance.

Let me tell you what would happen if someone in a war was killed; this may help you to understand better. Imagine that someone was running with a gun, shooting at the enemy. When he got shot himself and killed instantly, he would continue to run at his enemy because his awareness would not have changed, even though he was in his light body. The only thing that would surprise him, at first, is he would run straight through his enemy. In fact, he would be able to pass through anything in the physical world. He would more than likely panic, not realising he was dead or transmigrated. At this point, there are helpers to explain to him what has happened. How do I know you can pass through anything in the physical world?

I first came out of my body years ago when I was at work. I was looking down at myself from about 10 feet or 3 metres, watching myself work quite normally. I must admit I found this rather strange, but I soon found myself back to normal.

The second time it happened, I was on holiday and found myself out again, but I was going into a building with my physical body. For a moment, I wondered what would happen, but to my amazement, I found myself passing through the wall just above the doorway that my body was passing through. Many people have out-of-body experiences, but they are afraid to talk about them because others may think they are making it up.

Look over there to the right; here comes a flock of geese. They are hard to see against the darkened sky as they blend in with the brisk, moving clouds. Listen to their calling, which will help you focus on them as they fly in that arrow formation. Apparently, it is the most efficient way for a body of birds to fly. Oh good, it looks as though they are going to land. Watch – it's the bit I like to see. I am sure this is where many got the idea to water ski from. See, they're just breaking formation, and this is where the fun starts. Here they come, feet out in front, wings spread out wide, a little adjustment to get themselves level and they're water skiing on their webbed feet. I'm sure they have a smile on their faces. Ha, look at that one on the far right! He's really going fast. See, he's just overtaken the one next to him! He's looking round at him as to say, "I'm better than you." That's it, all down now. That was enjoyable, wasn't it?

They are all gathering together now like a huddle of women having a good natter at the shops. Notice how the light reflects off the rippling water as the wind makes strange patterns on the surface. It's amazing how all species of life have some way of communicating with their own kind.

A WALK IN THE RAIN

Chapter 15

Looking down through the worlds

S hall we walk along the water's edge round to that jetty where the boat house is nestling in the cluster of laurel trees? Have you ever seen geese landing on the ice? If you ever get the chance to see it, you'll have a laugh. One year I came up here in the dead of winter and some geese came in to land.

As you can imagine, they were sliding all over the place. One slid along on the ice perfectly until he reached the water, and as soon as his feet touched the water, he flipped head over tail. You should have seen the expression on his face once he had righted himself. He must have heard me laughing because he gave me a look then swam off with the hump.

Many people envy birds. They have the best of both worlds. They can walk on the ground, fly wherever they wish and some can even swim. But it is the flying that causes the main envy.

When you are in the Body of Light, the mode of movement is similar to flying. You can travel at tremendous speed because, unlike on Earth, there is no resistance or wind. One thing to remember is although we on Earth are unable to see the next level up, which is the second level, the Emotional world, those on the second level can see us on the physical, those on third level can see the second, and so on. Therefore, those in the Light Bodies on the Emotional level can see what is happening in the physical world, and this is not by accident, as you will discover.

The other thing that needs to be understood is how one creates things on this second level of consciousness. It is done by thought; in other words, what you think happens. Fortunately, we have dropped the five passions or traps; otherwise, there would be conflicts of opposites on this level.

That looks like Leaner walking this way. I wonder what he's doing. What are you laughing at? Leaner? Yes that's what everyone calls him. Funny, really. You see, he was walking up Abbots Hill one really windy day so he had to lean forwards into the wind to stop himself being blown backwards. Then, all of a sudden, the wind stopped and he fell flat on his face and rolled down the hill, so ever since then we've called him Leaner.

"Hi, Leaner! What on earth are you doing over here?"

"Just popped over to pay my son's mooring fee before it runs out. He keeps forgetting to bring it. What brings you out?"

"Oh, just out for a walk. What's up with your face, Leaner? It looks a bit swollen."

"Toothache! Can't get it seen to until Wednesday."

"Have you tried vinegar and pepper? Get some brown paper, soak it in vinegar, then sprinkle pepper on it. Place it on the spot that hurts. It burns like hell and takes the pain away! It's the best remedy there is."

"Right! I'll try that when I get home. Thanks."

"Bye, Leaner."

Now, where were we? Oh yes. One of the main purposes in the emotional world is to prepare you for the next rebirth. There are some who think you are judged for your behaviour in the last life, but it is not a judgement; it is an assessment of the preferences you have made. After this assessment, the requirements of your next life are worked out. If you remember about the circles, some were completed, others were not and some had just been started. There are records kept of all your circles completed, uncompleted and to be commenced.

It is the duty of the Lords of Time to allocate what period of time you enter and what circumstances you need to experience in accordance with your circles. For instance, say one of your experiences was to save a boy from drowning in a life which occurred three or four lifetimes ago. For you, this circle must at some time be completed. There may be an opportunity to complete this in your next re-birth. As I said earlier, some of these circles overlap centuries of time and involve many people. For the likes of you and me to comprehend the immensity of this mechanism of circles of time and opposites, the organisation and manipulation of its complexity is almost impossible. Therefore, until you can prove this for yourself, and no doubt it will be given to you if you really wish it, you will have to trust what is said.

You could ask the Master of the Dream to help you. Who is the Master of the Dream? All I can say at the moment is that it is the living conscious spirit, the substance of the dream. For you to try and understand such things at the moment would be like me asking you to catch the wind.

A WALK IN THE RAIN

Chapter 16

The Second World

The ground is quite soggy. The land here is mainly clay, and that is one reason they chose to flood the valley, but the strange thing is just up the hill where we came from, there is a rock formation, hence the old quarry there. Someone is feeding the geese. I am surprised there are no ducks today. It looks like Horse feeding them. No, not a horse! He works for the water company. He got the name Horse because he's always saying nay instead of no. They call his son Pony. Ted and I were going to call him Cart so when they came into the Mudhole, we could say here comes Horse and Cart, but we decided not to.

My sense of humour has got me into some tight corners sometimes and out of them at other times. One day, when I was a young man, I was driving in Understone town centre when I had a bit of a tadoo with another motorist. For some reason which I have forgotten, I was in front of him, making "big head" signs to him. Unfortunately, I got caught by the traffic lights and had to stop. He got out of his car and came up to me. I thought the doors were locked, but no, to my horror, he opened my door and was quite angry. Luckily, I saw the funny side and started to laugh, which got him by surprise. "What's funny?" he said. I told him I thought the doors were locked. Luckily he saw the funny side too and started laughing with me, and we parted friends. Phew, that was close.

Right, back to discussing the Emotional World. I suppose you are wondering where this world is. It starts here on Earth and stretches out to space, consisting of many levels according to your state of awareness. Those with little knowledge or interest in spiritual affairs prefer to stay near the Earth world, while others can move to higher regions where they can study Art, Music and Spiritual Truths and also use the imagination, the Creative Gem, to create things because what you imagine will materialise.

Now listen, all the inventions on Earth have come from this level of consciousness. When the time for man to achieve flight was right according to the Dream, it was given to the Wright Brothers. Apparently, one of them was shown in a dream how to construct the wing of the aeroplane. I think you will find this is a recorded fact. Everything that is invented is meant to be at that given time within the circles of time and destiny of the world, but man, in his arrogant ignorance, takes the credit for himself. To those who know, it is just the playing of the dream.

I would like you to understand that each world controls the world below. This is one reason each world can observe the one below. Each world is looked after by a Lord or Ruler who has immense powers, and if you take time to search such matters, you will learn more about them.

One thing that does concern most people is when children transmigrate. Firstly, it is in accordance with these circles, and helpers in the Emotional world know when the child's time is right and they are waiting for them. Children have a wonderful time in this world because they are adept at using their Creative Gem, their imagination. Another thing to note is that when there is a mass of people transmigrating through either a war or some disaster, there are always workers ready to receive those passing over to the second world.

Nearly there! See how nicely the place is kept, with the grass cut and the flower beds neat and tidy and filled with brightly coloured flowers. There must be about 70 boats tied up. No motor boats are allowed because of the risk of pollution. The wind surfers have to go at the other end of the reservoir to avoid any accidents with the sailing boats. I'm not a boat person myself, although I did hire a canal boat some years ago, which was quite relaxing until I fell in the river. I was standing on the back of the boat and my friend was driving into a lock, but he hit the side of the lock and I fell in. I am a good swimmer, so it was OK, but to top it all, I then had a shower on the boat and after I had finished, I grabbed what I thought was talc powder. I sprinkled it all over me and immediately came out in red blotches. Still not realising what I had done, I came out on deck and the others commented on the red blotches. I told them it happened when I put the talc on, and they said we didn't have any talc. I discovered, now don't laugh, that it was Ajax powder for cleaning the toilet, so I had to have another shower. Mind you, that's the cleanest I've ever been! I made them all promise not to tell anyone in the village as I didn't want the nick name Ajax! Luckily they all kept their promise! Here we are; this is the boat house.

A WALK IN THE RAIN

Chapter 17

Looking at the Traps

We have to wipe our boots well before we go inside. They keep this place spotless. They have a guided tour round the treatment works and pumping station once a month. Some schools bring their pupils here for educational trips. Over here are some of the pictures before they flooded the valley. As you can see, it was quite a nice wooded area. Those two cottages down in the valley, as well as the land, belonged to the Woods family. When the water company bought this land, the Woods sold the rest of the land to the Richardsons and moved away, down to the West Country I believe.

The Simmons lived in the nearest one. They moved to Norfolk once it was sold. There's a funny story about their son Ralf. He was a nice boy but easily led. He worked for the local builders called Buildwright as a labourer. The trouble with Ralf was that he had a bee in his bonnet about money; he always wanted a lot of money. So the other boys told him that there was a job advertised in Upperfield for a bulletproof vest tester at six hundred pounds a week. Ralf, being the person he was, jumped at the idea. The boys, including Ted's son, said they would arrange an interview for him. They got one of their mates in Upperfield to pretend to be the interviewer. Ralf fell for it, went for the interview and was offered the job. Ralf came back and said he was giving in his notice. When the boss found out what he was going to do, although he thought it was rather funny, he called the boys in to find out what was going on. Ralf was quite upset that it had been a joke, so the boys were ordered to buy Ralf's lunch for a week. Mind you, it didn't stop them playing some other jokes on Ralf. The one about how to be a spin bowler was good, but that's another story.

I'll just show you the club bar and lounge while we're here, through the door on the right. Quite a posh place and it has a wonderful view. Over there behind the swaying poplar trees lies Fairy Wood, and from this side, if you look over the dam, you can see right down the valley. That large round tower is the overflow which leads to the river. Ready? We'll walk down to the village by the proper footpath, and we'll be passing my old primary school. I still remember it well.

As you can imagine, as you are passing through the Maze of Time and Opposites, you are slowly working your way back to the Dreamer. Therefore, there must be a rather large variation in awareness within the population of our world. If you can understand that we are ever coming and going through reincarnation and slowly becoming more spiritually aware, there must be this variation. Unfortunately, it is this variation which has brought about many conflicts between man caused by one of the five passions or traps, Lust, Anger, Greed, Attachment and Vanity. Although these appear quite simple, they have many tentacles which work against your unfoldment, and some are so subtle that you do not even know they have entered your state of mind or outlook. It would be very interesting and beneficial to look at these five passions and their tentacles in more detail.

Lust can catch you out because it is very subtle in its approach. It normally comes in the form of longing for something that is not a necessity for survival. There are many under the power of drugs and alcohol, rich food and, of course, money and erotic sex. Money and sex are the downfall of many a man in a position of power.

Anger is common to most people, and it is getting a foothold with road rage, air rage and football supporters' rage. It can turn into hatred, causing mass destruction of life and property. At this stage, one has totally lost respect for others. But anger's tentacles are far more subtle. It can start by talking to others in an offensive way, being impatient, finding fault and criticising others in an ill-mannered way. Once anger takes hold of someone, it can turn into hatred, and this can fester for many years before exploding into some outrageous act of cruelty.

Greed has grown more since man has become more affluent. The old saying "The more one has, the more one wants" sums this up nicely. Its tentacles are quite obvious. Robbery is one of the main manifestations, trying to get something for nothing. Lying and corruption by bribery also come under Greed. This passion makes one think only of oneself and can make a person become very deceitful and manipulative just to get what they want or to stop others from obtaining something.

Attachment is a very clever trickster because it can creep up on you without any sign until the time comes to give something up or lose it. Some people can become attached to all sorts of causes. They may think they are doing something worthwhile. Whether it is or not is not important, but they are trapped by their attachment and it will take over their lives; some lose all sense of logic. Attachment can fix the mind in a groove which is hard to escape from. It can be so subtle that it can make a person collect things and keep their attention upon those possessions. A question they should ask themselves is whether they can take their collection with them at the end.

We'll take the right hand fork up here. There are some lovely azaleas just round the corner behind that hedge.

Lastly, there is Vanity.

A WALK IN THE RAIN

Chapter 18

More of the Traps

*T*here we are. What do you think of that show of colour? Wonderful! Even the primroses are still managing to sprout their last blooms, with the bluebells in the background. It is a sight for sore eyes. The one thing that amazes me is no matter what colour flowers are mixed together, they never clash. Take these azaleas. There are five different colours, with the primroses and the bluebells, yet they all blend in perfectly. Is it the green foliage that is able to fuse these colours together? If you tried to mix these colours yourself, they would clash so badly you wouldn't like to look at the result.

There's the Lodge House. We'll give our number back to God Bless. He never says goodbye; he always replies, "God Bless." Mind you, that's much nicer than saying Good Bye! He's not religious in any way, but for some reason, he has always said God Bless, no matter who people are. It's funny what little quirks we have. Some people acquire unusual movements or strange noises, just like Charlie's grunt. Have you ever met people who repeat your last word of a sentence? For example, you say, "Nice day," and they reply, "Day." You say, "Going for a walk," and they reply, "Walk." I find it quite frustrating. If you ever do come across someone with a quirk like that, the best thing to do is the same thing back. Mind you, if they have this quirk really badly, you could end up just saying one word all the time — a nice day, day, day, day, day! You see what I mean?

"Hi, God Bless! Here's our number. We had a nice view of the geese landing. See you later. Bye."

"God Bless," replies God Bless.

The fifth trap is Vanity. You will find this is the hardest passion to overcome because it focuses your attention on yourself. Its tentacles are the most subtle of all. There are many people in the limelight who become trapped by vanity, unable to give up the attention bestowed on them. Those who look down on poor people or like to show off their wealth, as well as those who brag about helping others, are also under the trap of Vanity. Anything that is done to draw attention to oneself or to make oneself look wonderful is Vanity. This also catches out many spiritually seeking people when they think they are in some way better than those who are not, but they themselves are not aware that we are all where we are by the Law of Opposites.

If you imagine planting five trees close to one another and each one is labelled Lust, Anger, Greed, Attachment or Vanity, their roots would all intertwine. This is precisely how they work. If they cannot get their way, they normally resort to Anger.

Most of the spiritual views look upon these passions or traps as evil, but they are only the negative side of the opposites. Although they are destructive, they are not evil; they are a necessity for without them, there could not be the opposites.

Turn left at the end of the drive, back onto the main road. We'll go past the old primary school.

The opposites are, if you remember, Forgiveness, Contentment, Detachment, Humility and Chastity. Now this is one thing a lot of people with spiritual interests do not realise: the five passions are a lot stronger than the five virtues. There is a logical reason for this; although many would not agree, the Dreamer's plan of things is based on mathematical logic. In fact, everything created is of a mathematical nature because the Sound is only maths in motion creating beauty. We'll have a look at this later.

The five passions are stronger because they are the ones that need to be dropped from your preferences; therefore, it would not be logical to have them easy to overcome. That is why you are ever being confronted by these passions. Although I have knowledge of their workings, I still fall into their traps myself. The one advantage of this is that I can become aware of my behavior quickly and try to change it.

Notice this lovely old brick pavement with the ornate railings. Although it only goes as far as the crossroads, it is very pleasing to the eye. That's my old primary school. It hasn't changed much, just new plastic windows and a new front porch. The headmistress was Miss Croucher, a rather small woman but extremely stern. She had those old-fashioned plaited buns, one over each ear, and she wore thick glasses perched on the end of her nose. She would have made a great E.T. in Spielberg's film. My early schooldays were a nightmare, me being somewhat of a rascal and my twin sister being more of a goody-goody. I spent most of my time standing in the corner. Miss Croucher had a pet cockatoo in her house next to the school. Her old house is no longer there as they built those new houses about ten years ago. If you were good, she used to let you go and feed the cockatoo as a reward. My sister got quite friendly with the bird, but alas, in all the five years I spent at the school, I knew every corner of the building in detail but never saw that cockatoo!

A WALK IN THE RAIN

Chapter 19

The Turning Point

*I*f you can recall, the overriding rule of the opposites and the creation *of the Sound and Light, including us as soul, is that everything must return to its origin. Therefore, there must be a point when we turn our attention towards the Dreamer via spiritual interests. Unfortunately, this is where people's vanity tends to creep in when they compare their spiritual interests with others'. Do not listen to others' preferences. It is for you to come to your own. Only you can compare through your experiences.*

There are many spiritual activities, and each one has its purpose in developing your preferences. As your preferences move from the five passions towards the five virtues, you will find that you are also growing in wisdom, power and freedom. You will notice that the average person looks upon spiritual groups as abnormal. This is because they are stuck in the illusion of being normal and safe. When you draw away from the run of the mill, you will find you have gained a freedom from the claws of formality and therefore have gained power over that lure to conform to the masses. Hence you have gained wisdom. From this point on, each reincarnation leads your circles ever closer to the Dreamer, and you grow in wisdom, power and freedom. You may also find that in each life from then on, the number of people in your life will slowly decrease as your personal circles decrease.

The first shop we come to is the butcher's. It used to belong to Mr White, rather a happy chap, who always made you welcome. He was well-known for his home-made sausages. People came from all over to buy them. One day, something very strange happened. His wife disappeared, leaving no note or anything to suggest what might have happened to her. The police made extensive inquiries but to no avail. Some say she ran off with a chap in Wiggleford; others reckon he bumped her off and put her in his sausages! I'm sure she ran off with someone, but I've never eaten a sausage since. His business went downhill after that, so he sold up and moved north. I hope I haven't put you off sausages! I wonder whether you will remember this story next time you buy some!

Let's have a look at some of the spiritual steps towards the Dreamer. Mediums are aware that life exists after transmigration. They also help people who have lost their loved ones. A good medium can really comfort relatives and friends. If contact is made and there is no doubt that it is that person whom they have been trying to contact, this also brings about a belief in life after death. This, in turn, sows a seed in their consciousness which may be of some help to them in their next reincarnation. The way this contact is made is by telepathy, thought or seeing their subject in their light body.

If you recall, I explained that on the second or emotional level, everything is created by thought. Mediums are trained to read these thought patterns, and some even see pictures of their subject as they were when they passed over. The reason why some make contact and others do not is that there are several levels on the second world. Some like to stay near the Earth and their family, whilst others who are more advanced move to the high levels to study, for example.

Astrology is quite an interesting subject, although I do not have much knowledge of how to work out people's charts. It teaches that life is influenced by the planets and this occurs by magnetic inputs brought about by the note or sound coming from each planet. This, in turn, can be made to echo off other planets, creating sacred geometry patterns of sound and light as the planets move in their preordained orbits. What people do not realise is this – now mark what I say! What's on the outside is also on the inside. This applies even to the smallest creature. You are governed by the planets on the inside, which, in turn, are governed by the planets on the outside. It sounds baffling but it really is quite simple; it only appears complicated!

No doubt you have seen a hologram? It is only light reflecting to make the image look as though it's 3-D. Remember everything is Sound and Light. Light reflects off the Sound and produces a hologram. If one takes a hologram and smashes it into a hundred pieces, each piece will be a complete replica of that hologram. You as soul are a hologram of the Dream. Therefore, what is happening on the outside is happening on the inside and affects you according to your circles, which are based on the notes of the planets. In other words, you are governed by Sound and Light. Do you see what I mean when I said that free will is not so? It may need some thinking over. Even the five worlds on the outside are on the inside. Remember this well. It is important.

When you dream, you travel on one of these inner worlds, and things can happen which are not logical or possible on Earth. For example, you could be flying in the air doing breaststroke. Have you ever had a dream which was so funny you have woken up laughing, only to wonder, upon recalling it, what was so funny about it? If you remember, I said that the Wright Brothers were shown the secrets of flight in a dream. This means they were on the second level, the emotional world, at that time. Jesus said, "The way to Heaven is to go within." He was referring to these inner worlds, and it is in these inner worlds you can meet the Master of the Dream.

A WALK IN THE RAIN

Chapter 20

Some Spiritual Interests

*T*hat shop with the large bay window used to be Knights Stores many years ago. They sold everything from greengrocery to haberdashery, ironmongery, grocery, gardening equipment and toys. You name it, Knights had it! It was like walking into Aladdin's cave. Not many people had televisions in those days, so they went to Knights instead because he would open late in the summer. Although it looked a complete shambles, with boxes all over the place, old Mr Knight could put his finger on whatever you asked for. Not only that, it was a place for people to meet and discuss their problems or learn about the latest gossip. Alas, those days have gone. People are too much wrapped up in themselves, and communities are dying.

You may have heard of numerology. It is quite interesting. All events are connected to numbers. Even the alphabet is transformed into numbers from one to nine. For example, A B C D E F G H I = 1 2 3 4 5 6 7 8 9. Then J K L M

N O P Q R becomes 1 2 3 4 5 6 7 8 9 and so on. Numerologists believe that your name and date of birth have a significant meaning. They change your name into numbers. For instance, if your name was Mike Wooble, the letters M I K E W O O B L E would become 4 9 2 5 5 6 6 2 3 5, and added all together, these equal 47. These two numbers are then added together to become 11. Most numbers are added together until they become a single number, so 11 would then be added together to end up as 2. However, 11 is looked upon as a special number, so it can remain as 11. Once the name number has been reached, that number is analysed for future predictions. This also applies to your birth date. If you remember, I mentioned the Guardians of the Nine. This is closely linked with numerology but has to do with the sacred codes and sacred geometry infused with the Divine Octave.

Tarot cards are similar to numerology. These cards are in four divisions as follows: Cups, Wands, Swords and Coins. Each of these four sets has corresponding numbers from one to ten, with kings, queens, knights and pages. These are the major arcana. Also, there are a variety of others, six of which are Justice, Temperance, Strength, the Hermit, the Wheel of Fortune and the Hanged Man. These are known as the trump cards, and there are 22 of them. Having selected your cards, the reader places them in a special order known as a spread and predicts your future. Some tarot readers are very good, whilst others are not. These readers also have an aptitude for being psychic. They are able to either see a picture of the future or have intuition.

Lots of people endeavour to foresee the future then try to change it. It is far better just to live life and let the circles take you along your path. Those who struggle and fight life may find life hard and become unhappy or envy others. We all have crosses to bear. The sooner you grasp that they are only a series of opposites you must experience, the sooner you can make your comparisons and your preferences and the more quickly you will move along the path towards the Dreamer.

There are many more interests, too many to mention, but all have their purpose. Alas, however, they are all part of the Maze of Opposites and will not lead you out to true wisdom, power and freedom.

That old cottage next to the Post Office was occupied by an eccentric old chap called Raymond Smilton. He was known as Sweet Jar to the people he worked with at the water company. Apparently, and this is only what I've heard from God Bless and some of the other chaps who worked there, Raymond used to bring all his meals for the day in a large sweet jar. So what's strange about that? First he would work out what he was going to have for all his meals the next day. The top layer was breakfast; let's say it was egg, bacon and sausages. He would cook them the night before. Then there was the 10 o'clock break, and he may have had two jam sandwiches. Then there was lunch, and this may have consisted of cold potatoes, chicken, peas and carrots. After that, apple pie for dessert. Lastly, the 3 o'clock break, which could be some jam donuts.

Now here comes the strange part. Raymond would put all this into his sweet jar in the corresponding order. First, in would go the jam donuts, followed by the apple pie, then the cold potatoes, peas, carrots, chicken and the jam sandwiches and lastly the breakfast egg, bacon and sausages. At the appropriate time, he would open his sweet jar and with a spoon commence to eat his meal for that time of day. As you can imagine, no one would sit and eat with Raymond. Now you can see why they called him Sweet Jar. He transmigrated about eleven years ago, and the cottage was sold to a young couple who are away in Australia for two years. They reckon when they cleaned his cottage out, it was full of old used sweet jars. Blah – would you like a sweet?

A WALK IN THE RAIN

Chapter 21

The Secret

*T*he only way out of the Maze of Opposites is to find a spiritual teaching which connects you with the Sound and Light because the Sound and Light is the Dreamer in Motion. Also, the opposites of Sound and Light are silence and dark, which are basically nothing, and, as I have said, everything has come from nothing.

Please note what I say! The Dreamer creates from nothing by using its Gem, and the opposite to nothing is everything. Therefore, everything is the Dreamer in Its various forms.

Other spiritual teachings also have their opposites, such as God and the Devil, Good and Evil, but you will find none of these opposites leads to silence and darkness. Therefore, they will not lead you out of the Maze.

Many people in various teachings think they are the chosen ones, which feeds their vanity. Listen! We are all the chosen ones; otherwise, we would not exist.

We are a divine consciousness progressing back to the Dreamer, but Vanity and Attachment are the hardest and the final passions to overcome because you have to let go of the Self.

The shop over on the right is a craft shop. The lady who owns the shop, Miss Ellis, is an artist and very good, too. We'll pop over and have a look in the window at some of her paintings. Look, there's one of Fairy Wood. Notice how she managed to get the moss on the rocks looking life-like. It is very clever. That picture in the corner of the tiger is done by making little dots and nothing else. Artists are very good at using the Creative Gem.

My art teacher at the secondary school in Wiggleford was Mr Fry. Teachers in those days were very strict and did not have much of a sense of humour. As you can imagine, that was very hard for me to cope with. By now, you must have some idea how I tick. Well, Mr Fry didn't. Once we had to draw and paint pub signs. I just couldn't resist being a rascal, and within two minutes I had finished my sign. "Get on with your painting," ordered Mr Fry. "I've finished, sir," I replied. "Finished! Don't be stupid, boy," Mr Fry shouted at me. "No, I have finished sir," I responded. "Bring it here," Mr Fry growled, so I gave him my painting, which was a sheet of paper painted black all over. "What on earth is this supposed to be?" Mr Fry asked, glaring at me. Looking him straight in the eye, with the rest of the class on the edge of their seats, I replied, with a slight smirk on my face, "It's the Dark Night, sir." Have you ever waited for a volcano to go off? You could see the rage growing inside. I had made him look a fool in front of the class. That was my speciality at school. You may notice that my bottom is much flatter than most people's. That's the result of all the beatings with a slipper. My cheeky retort got me six of the best from Mr Fry. But there is a better one than that with the English teacher, Mr Springate, who was also the deputy head. It's about penguins. Well, that's got you guessing! You will just have to wait for a while!

We have established that the opposite of Sound and Light is darkness and silence. We have also discussed the existence of inner worlds. Now there's the strange thing: we have to leave the Light and Sound of this world and sit in the opposites, total silence and total darkness, to experience the Light and Sound of the Dreamer. Now remember this because I am going to explain how to contact this Sound and Light and the Master of the Dream in a moment. First, let's run through the important points we have discussed. It may be hard to understand, but everything has come from nothing. Listen and concentrate! The Dreamer was intelligence surrounded by silence and darkness. It manifests Itself by imagining Itself as Sound and Light. This is Its first creation. From there on, everything has its opposite and is governed by the Law of Opposites. Everything must return to its origin, consisting of a sacred code in conjunction with its seven notes and seven colours of the Sound and Light, with low and high notes, loud and soft, fast and slow, all organised into rhythms and harmonies. The code is a special mathematical formula determining the 365 days in a year, seven days in a week, the number of days in a month, in fact, the whole universe, but I will save that for another time.

The Sound manifested the Light, which was transformed into colours of light and dark shades, bright and dim. Next, magnetism, with positive and negative, repels and attracts, and by splitting these two apart, the Big Bang was created, producing our world of opposites for us to experience, so we are able to have comparisons by which to produce our preferences. The two important things which I have omitted are beauty and love because they have an opposite. They are a creation of the Dreamer and not the Dreamer Itself, as many believe.

A WALK IN THE RAIN

Chapter 22

Explaining the Master of the Dream

O h yes! About the penguins! My twin sister was quite bright. In fact, she was in the A stream and was made head girl. We have been talking about opposites; well, meet the opposite to my sister – me! Dyslexic, hair that had its own mind, reading and writing a nightmare, discipline (you're joking), mischievous, maths brilliant (my favourite subject).

There was one drawback. Because I couldn't read, I was unable to read the maths questions, so the teacher had to tell me. In the English lesson, we were asked to write a story. My story was about a factory which had something blocking its chimney and smoking the place out. One of the workers had to climb up the chimney's ladder to see what was blocking it, and when he got to the top, he found a penguin's nest. I know what you're thinking, so don't say it! You must realise that because I was dyslexic and unable to spell very well, only a magician could read my story.

I was in the woodwork class one day, making a three-legged stool with four legs, when I had orders to go to see Mr Springate, the English teacher.

When I arrived at his classroom, wondering what on earth I had done, he was taking English with the A stream, yes, my sister's class. On the blackboard, Mr Springate had written my story with the same spelling as my original essay. He asked whether I could read it to the class because no one else could. So I began to read it. Everyone was laughing because of the spelling, but when I came to the penguin's nest, they were in stitches. I was not embarrassed, however, and I still had my trump card to play. When they had settled down, Mr Springate said with a big smile on his face, "Don't you know penguins can't fly?" "Oh, yes, sir, but they are very good at climbing ladders," I replied. You think I got the slipper? No! I couldn't believe it. I had played my trump card AND got away with it, which was the first time ever. The next day I had to go and see the headmaster, and to my surprise, he said they had decided to make me a prefect. Things were looking up.

The time has come to discuss how we can find the way out of this Maze of Time and Opposites. Firstly, we know that the only two opposites that consist of nothing are the Sound and Light. Secondly, the Law of Opposites states that everything must return to its origin. Even the Light and Sound must return to their origin, which is the Dreamer. Are you with me so far?

Now, we need to contact the Sound and the Light on our way back to the Dreamer. The only way this can be achieved is by meeting the Master of the Dream. This is not an easy thing for me to explain, but I will try. The Sound and the Light are the Holy Spirit. It is the Dreamer in motion, which gives life to everything. It is aware of everything because everything is Itself. (For instance, you know what your big toe is doing, as well as your left eye, because they are part of you.) It is the first creation of the Dreamer which gives life to Its dream. It is this Sound and Light or Holy Spirit which is the Master of the Dream.

Jesus said, "Of myself I do nothing; it is the Father within." The Master of the Dream has always been with you and always will be. He also said, "The

Kingdom of Heaven is within…" It is the very life within. Therefore, it is essential that you go within to find the Master of the Dream, either by seeing the Light or hearing the Sound. This is done by bringing your full attention to the centre of the forehead, approximately between the eyebrows. There are several teachings that instruct their followers to concentrate on this point, but some are only trying to control the mind. The important thing is looking for the Light and listening for the Sound.

Everything has this Sound within. If you really concentrate while trying to go within and listen with concentrated attention to the silence, you may begin to hear a high-pitched sound which is very faint at first, but if you concentrate on this sound, you may find it grows louder. This is the Sound that runs through all life. The Light may appear at the spot between the eyebrows as a small blue light, and if you see that, you should concentrate on that light.

It is also possible to leave the human body at a point at the top of the head, but there are drawbacks. It is advisable to find the teachings of Sound and Light which teach the correct method of travelling in the inner worlds.

A WALK IN THE RAIN

Chapter 23

Trust It

O n the corner, there was a pub called the Anchor, but it was abandoned because of bad subsidence. Then one Saturday morning at about 10 o'clock, it disappeared into a large hole which had opened up, about forty feet deep and forty feet wide. They found that there was an underground river which had eaten away the earth. It took many lorry loads of hardcore to fill it in.

Then they grassed it over and it's been that way ever since.

That building over to the right, with all those lovely hanging baskets, is an estate agent. Property has gone up immensely in the last few years. The trouble is the young people in the village can't afford such prices, and village life is dying because of it. I think those hanging baskets are really wonderful, although I'm not a great gardener myself. At school I did not like gardening that much, and, what with my mischievous ways, it led to the biggest fright of my life. You see, Brian Clark and I decided to pull up the flowers and leave the weeds, just for devilment. Unfortunately, Mr Vallerson thought otherwise. He was a short little man, and when he gave you the slipper, it did not hurt too much. He called Brian and me over to the gardening shed and told me to wait outside while he sorted out Brian. Now Brian Clark was the biggest boy in the school. I heard Mr Vallerson say to him, "Bend over the bench." Then there was an almighty whack and Brian let out a painful yell, then another whack and another painful wail. I thought to myself, "What on earth is he hitting him with?" After three whacks and the painful yells from Brian, there was a shout of desperation: "No more, sir, no more!" As you can imagine, I was trembling in my boots. If he could do that to Brian, what on earth would he do to me? "Let that be a lesson to you, boy," Mr Vallerson said in a firm voice. "Your turn, young man. Inside." As I walked through the shed door, wondering whether I would ever walk out alive, there was Brian dancing around holding his bottom. "Right, lie across the bench." I almost stopped breathing as I saw him pick up a witch's broom. My legs were shaking, and my heart was pounding. This is the End! Then... a roar of laughter from both Mr Vallerson and Brian. What was so funny? I was about to get the beating of my life and there they were, laughing! "Stand up! That made you think, boy." "What sir?" I asked. "I'll show you what went on," and Mr Vallerson raised the witch's broom and brought it down on the bench, and Brian gave out a yell. Yes, I'd been fooled, but the relief was wonderful. It took me a few moments to come back to reality before I saw the funny side.

That fright had done more good than all the other beatings put together. Ah, but he hadn't finished. "Four weeks doing needlework with the girls may do you some good!" "Four weeks with the girls, sir? I'll be the laughing stock of the school!" "Yes, lad you will." A smile beamed across his face.

Many people who have spiritual interests believe that God will give them the good things in life. In some cases, it looks as though their wishes have been granted. What they do not understand is they may have started a new circle of opposites. The only reason to become interested in spiritual affairs is to connect with the Sound and Light and to complete your outstanding circles. Now there can be a speeding up of your circles, so instead of things becoming better, there is a possibility that things will become unsettled for a short period of time. This is a blessing. Although some of your circles are speeding up, the danger is you are still making new circles, which, if you remember, once locked in time must be completed.

The best course of action is to surrender yourself to the Master of the Dream, whether you understand it or not. If you can recall, I said you should trust it. Just state it but mean what you say, then surrender to the Master of the Dream, which is the living Sound and Light. You may notice that whatever you do returns to you in a short period of time. This makes you become aware of your circles and how intricate they can be.

A WALK IN THE RAIN

Chapter 24

Dreams

We'll turn up this alleyway on the right. There's a quaint old cottage up here. It is over three hundred years old, and you can stand up only in between the oak beams. There! See how low the windows are; you have to bend down to look out of them. The well in the front garden is original and is about 150 feet deep. Now here's something people don't know: when they build a brick well, they build it from the top down – no, really! First they build about 3 feet of brickwork on the ground and let it dry. Then they dig inside and the brick wall slides down. They repeat this over and over. As they get deeper, they make a platform half way across the well, so one man can pass a bucket of earth up to the next level with the men safely inside the brick well – quite ingenious, don't you think?

Apparently, it was the cottage for the coachman for The Grange, which was a large house owned by a lord, but it was sold some years ago after falling into disrepair and a housing estate was built there. If we carry on through this small copse, we'll come to the old brick fields.

It's important that you try to stop making fresh circles. The main culprit is being attached to people and events. The most successful way of relieving yourself of these burdens is to become indifferent to life. This is not an easy task. Firstly, it is advisable to look at other people's actions as being only conditions of their circles and having nothing to do with you. Being indifferent doesn't mean you do not care about people. It is still important that you show respect to others but without interfering or giving advice unless you are asked. Even then, be careful because people's problems are theirs, connected to their circles.

You will find, as you progress, some relationships will drop away and new ones will start. You will also notice more and more that there seems to be a guiding hand leading you. If you come to a situation that is stopping your progress in one direction, do not fight it. The way that is best for you will open. Remember, TRUST IT. It is working for your benefit and not your desires. Remember – not your desires.

Here we are. You wouldn't believe this was once a brick field. Wiggleford Council bought the land and landscaped it and stocked the lake with fish. Several fishing clubs hire it from the council. Security is very tight to stop children getting in. This footpath goes round the boundary and comes out by the village pond where we saw the ducks.

You may find that you start having vivid dreams. Most people dismiss dreams as nothing, but dreams are far more important than one can imagine. They can also come from one of the four levels of consciousness. But first let's have a look at the way some dreams help balance a person's personality. Let's take a person who is weak in strength and personality. He would more than likely have dreams of being the opposite – strong and a hero.

Other dreams can warn of some experience coming. For example, people at work know I am interested in such things, although I do not say much. A new chap had been with the firm for a few weeks. He spoke to his workmate about a re-

occurring dream. His workmate advised him to have a chat with me. His dream was as follows:

He had two pets, a cat and a small dog. They both went out into the garden but never came back. When he went out to find them, he found they were both dead on the lawn, next to the garden shed. He would put his hand on the shed and a rat would grab his hand. He would try to kill the rat by pulling the rat's mouth, but the mouth just kept stretching. What did I make of that?

I told him he had been given a blessing and a chance to put something right. I didn't know him, and this is how I explained it to him. The two pets represent two loved ones. Going out into the garden means they are losing their love for him, and if it continues, the love will die. The cause of this is his mouth, which is getting larger, indicating anger. The man was gobsmacked and explained to me that he was always having arguments with his sixteen-year-old daughter, and things were getting worse. I explained that if he did not heed this warning, he would lose his daughter and his marriage. I also told him that this advice was not mine and I had no concern in the matter; it was from a higher source, whether he believed it or not. He took my explanation, sat down with his family and sorted it out. By doing this, he saved his marriage and his relationship with his daughter.

As you can see, things are not always as we assume. Man is full of vanity, and it is his vanity which keeps him away from the Master of the Dream.

Dreams can also be a way of testing you on your preferences. In the physical world, we do some things because society expects us to act that way, but in dreams, we can react in a more responsive way according to our consciousness and preferences.

A WALK IN THE RAIN

Chapter 25

End of the Walk, Beginning of Freedom

*T*here are some fishermen over there by those tall reeds trying to camouflage themselves with their green umbrellas. They are like the golfers: no matter what the weather, they are out there. Those two fishing umbrellas are like miniature millennium domes. That one over by those two large willows – can you see it's got clear plastic sides? That looks cosy. Some fishermen sit there all day watching a small float bobbing up and down. Maybe that's where the nodding of the head comes from. For yes, I reckon one fisherman shouted to another fisherman, "Have you caught anything yet?" and as he replied, "Yes," his head was bobbing up and down with the float. Hence the beginning of nodding the head for yes!

Can you see how man is ever using his Creative Gem to improve things such as fishing umbrellas? Now this may be of interest: although man is ever improving and inventing things, the circles of time are very similar to those centuries ago, except we may be more comfortable. It is the five passions that lock the circles of opposites, and they have been the same since the first man.

There's the village pond just behind those tall poplar trees, so we are nearly home.

As you may have noticed, our conversation has been a series of opposites, sometimes serious and sometimes light-hearted. You may have learnt that you only get out of life what you put into it. Now this is for you to understand.

Firstly, no one else can make you happy, only yourself. There is only you and the Dreamer within. If you are angry, it is because you have become attached to some event. Everything in your life comes from you. If you feel sad because you have lost a loved one, that sadness comes from you and no one else.

Secondly, you own nothing whatsoever except your preferences. Everything on Earth belongs to time, and it will claim it when and where the circles demand it, so why struggle to collect so much?

Thirdly, you are not in any position to judge others. They are equal to you as soul. Their circles may take them in opposite directions to your liking, so let things be as they are.

Fourthly, remember there must always be the opposites. The world cannot function without them.

Now the big question is love. Most teachings say God is Love, but the Dreamer is pure intelligence and the highest form of intelligence is mathematics. Where or how this intelligence came into being is a mystery that is beyond our understanding. The evidence is undisputable, but its secret will frighten mankind. What is love and what is its purpose? Many think love is being kind and so on, but it is not. This is the perfect preference you have gained. Love is a feeling of desire. It is a movement inside. It is glue, created to bring about attention and maintain it. It is the glue that binds all creation together. Relationships will only flourish if love binds the two together. This love can be for each other or it can bring people together through their love of the same hobby and so forth. Love and the Gem of Imagination are tied together. It is the feeling of love which keeps the Gem's attention on Its creation. If it loses interest, it is because it has lost its love for it.

Most people have their attention on material things, but, as I have said, nothing belongs to you. The only thing that you have is inside yourself and that is the Gem, consisting of Sound and Light and the Master of the Dream. If you place your attention upon this, it will run your life according to your wishes if your preferences are correct. On the point of responsibility, it is also connected to love. If someone loves a garden or a car, for example, they take care of it and look after it. In other words, they become responsible for it and cherish it.

Now here lies a secret. Most people think they are responsible for themselves. The Master of the Dream is responsible for you. It has been running your lives all the time without your knowing, bringing you to the point of perfect preferences. So you surrender yourself to It. It is the living Dreamer, the Divine Father within you. As soul, therefore, to whom or what are you responsible? You look puzzled! You are responsible to the Dreamer. It created you. You exist because It loves you. Its attention is upon you, and It is responsible for you. Do you agree?

Therefore, you should love and be responsible back. It is a marriage between you and the Dreamer. Once your preferences reflect the five virtues of forgiveness, chastity, humility, detachment and contentment, and are welded into the Gem, and you are prepared to give yourself to and for the Dreamer and Its creation, you will become a Worker of the Dream, the Lover of All because all is the Dreamer. At this point, you will never have to return to this world of opposites. You will live in the Dream worlds of Sound and Light, working for the whole of the Dream. You will have earned wisdom, freedom and power, ever in the presence of the Dreamer and its love. So remember, believe in it, trust in it and surrender to it.

Here! We are back at the pond. The ducks are still there. Have you enjoyed the walk? I hope you are not too wet!

If you would like to have more spiritual knowledge, I would recommend you look up https://www.Eckankar.org.

Printed in Great Britain
by Amazon